**The Arnold and Caroline Rose Monograph Series of the
American Sociological Association**

Manufacturing green gold

Capital, Labor, and Technology in the Lettuce Industry

D1447862

Other books in the series

J. Milton Yinger, Kiyoshi Ikeda, Frank Laycock, and Stephen J. Cutler: *Middle Start: An Experiment in the Educational Enrichment of Young Adolescents*

James A. Geschwender: *Class, Race, and Worker Insurgency: The League of Revolutionary Black Workers*

Paul Ritterband: *Education, Employment, and Migration: Israel in Comparative Perspective*

John Low-Beer: *Protest and Participation: The New Working Class in Italy*

Orrin E. Klapp: *Opening and Closing: Strategies of Information Adaptation in Society*

Rita James Simon: *Continuity and Change: A Study of Two Ethnic Communities in Israel*

Marshall B. Clinard: *Cities with Little Crime: The Case of Switzerland*

Steven T. Bossert: *Tasks and Social Relationships in Classrooms: A Study of Instructional Organization and Its Consequences*

David R. Heise: *Understanding Events: Affect and the Construction of Social Action*

Richard E. Johnson: *Juvenile Delinquency and Its Origins: An Integrated Theoretical Approach*

Ida Harper Simpson: *From Student to Nurse: A Longitudinal Study of Socialization*

Stephen P. Turner: *Sociological Explanation as Translation*

Joseph Chamie: *Religion and Fertility: Arab-Christian-Muslim Differentials*

Janet W. Salaff: *Working Daughters of Hong Kong: Female Filial Piety or Intrafamilial Power?*

Manufacturing green gold

Capital, Labor, and Technology in the Lettuce Industry

William H. Friedland
Amy E. Barton
University of California, Santa Cruz
Robert J. Thomas
University of Michigan, Ann Arbor

Cambridge University Press
Cambridge
London   New York   New Rochelle
Melbourne   Sydney

Published by the Press Syndicate of the University of Cambridge
The Pitt Building, Trumpington Street, Cambridge CB2 1RP
32 East 57th Street, New York, NY 10022, USA
296 Beaconsfield Parade, Middle Park, Melbourne 3206, Australia

First published 1981

Printed in the United States of America

Library of Congress Cataloging in Publication Data
Friedland, William H.
Manufacturing green gold.
 (The Arnold and Caroline Rose monograph series of the American Sociological
Association)
Bibliography: p.
Includes index.
1. Lettuce industry – United States.
I. Barton, Amy E.   II. Thomas, Robert J.
III. Title.   IV. Series: Arnold and Caroline
Rose monograph series of the American
Sociological Association.
HD9235.L42U54   338.1'7552'0973   81–9959
ISBN 0 521 24284 3 hard covers   AACR2
ISBN 0 521 28584 4 paper back

Contents

Preface

We are concerned with the analysis of a specific segment of the agricultural production system of the United States. The chapters that follow will examine, in some detail, the ways in which social groups interact with one another in the making of a common food in American society: iceberg lettuce. The major questions informing the research, however, extend beyond the specific features of lettuce production. Rather we are interested more generally with the factors influencing the organization of industrial production. In particular, how are new methods of production formulated? What forces determine the acceptance or rejection of new technologies?

We seek answers to these questions by focusing on a major agricultural industry currently moving in the direction of large-scale changes in work organization. Thus the more general questions lend a specific focus to the analysis: What factors led to the development of a mechanical lettuce harvester? What consequences might be expected as a result of harvest mechanization?

This monograph is also explicitly focused on two additional and distinct kinds of activities. First, it is directed toward contributing to the emergence of a *sociology of agriculture,* which we expect to locate, in turn, in a broader body of knowledge and theory – *the comparative analysis of production systems*. In this approach the goal is to integrate the analysis of social systems involving agricultural production with a broader body of theory and research concerned with production. We are especially interested in addressing sociology and political economy as disciplines. Each of these disciplines has both relevant bodies of literature that have been drawn upon and intellectual questions to which a sociology of agriculture can contribute.

Second, beyond disciplinary involvements, but with a related set of concerns, we believe the analysis of concrete social systems requires some form of *application*. Our strategy here undertakes empirical analysis to deal with the social consequences deriving from real and potential changes in the system of production. Utilizing the analysis of lettuce production, we intend to develop specific social projections of the outcomes of a particular technological change, on the one hand, while working toward the development of a more generalizable methodology of social projection, on the other.

Many social and natural scientists have been engaged recently in seeking applications of knowledge to the improvement of society. Yet the mainstream positivistic traditions of modern social science, on the whole, have rejected this approach, arguing not only for "value-freedom" but for the insulation of academicians and intellectuals from the political process. Other traditions in the sciences and social sciences, however, have argued for application of social knowledge toward social improvement. In this respect, although insisting on the need for solid, objective analysis of the social order, we believe it important that scientists and social scientists clarify the value assumptions that underlie their work.

One assumption we make is that the sciences, social and natural, as well as the actors involved in these operations, can and should apply their knowledge to concrete situations. The notion of a "detached" science seems naïve to us; if scientists discover knowledge and simply cast it into the world, it will still have consequences. This leads, therefore, to our second assumption: The discovery of knowledge has social consequences. The actors, as well as the institutions in which they function, bear responsibility for these consequences, even if the actors do not personally implement them. Third, the production and implementation of scientific knowledge constitutes social intervention. In contrast to positivist notions about a "value-free" science, we believe that science is a value-laden and structured activity used most often to legitimate existing relations of power and control. Scientific knowledge can, however, be used to counter relations of inequality if advanced on behalf of disadvantaged groups or social categories. Thus the process of social intervention can and should be geared toward the improvement of society, and this study explicitly is concerned with finding an application in that direction.

This study may prove somewhat unconventional both in terms of the orientations previously outlined and by its "location" within current intellectual paradigms in the social sciences and in existing bodies of knowledge.

The major underlying theoretical categories and concepts are drawn primarily, but not exclusively, from Marxian theory. Because of the proliferation of Marxian and neo-Marxian theories in recent years and the often overlapping, and sometimes contradictory, meanings laid on basic ideas, we will attempt to provide definitions and operationalizations of concepts as we proceed. We realize that, for example, "mode of production," "social relations of production," and "labor process" are often vague, ill defined, or used as a shorthand for communication between initiates to the theory informing them. In order to communicate with the mainstream of sociology as well as to others working in the Marxian tradition, we will endeavor to make these ideas clearer.

We recognize, however, the need to integrate the work of other social scientists where appropriate. Of particular importance are theories of economic organization and bureaucracy. We will interact, therefore, with Max Weber's contributions as we analyze relations between political and economic institutions, for example, the relationship between publicly funded research organizations such as the University of California and private, large-scale, capitalist enterprises.

Although the work undertaken here could conceivably be integrated with rural and industrial sociology, that is, constitute an intersection between them, it addresses a constellation of issues that both fields have avoided with considerable alacrity. As we will show later, rural sociology has preferred to define its field of work rather narrowly, almost totally ignoring the analysis of agricultural production. Approaches to the organizations and social relationships embodied in agricultural production have been largely indirect, focusing on the processes of technological innovation and diffusion rather than examining the material or organizational bases for change in the organization of production (Nolan et al. 1975; Friedland 1979).

Because agriculture has been normatively viewed, within the broader discipline of general sociology, as "belonging" to the rural sociologists, both general and industrial sociology have avoided the examination of agriculture. By locating the work as we have, we hope readers will be able to transcend "normal" jurisdictional boundaries within the discipline and treat the work as intended – as a substantive analysis of the social organization of production.

Acknowledgments

Research reported in this study was supported by the National Science Foundation through its program on Ethics and Values in Science and Values in Science and Technology, Grant No. OSS 77-24678; the Agricultural Experiment Station of the University of California, Davis; and the Faculty Research Committee of the University of California, Santa Cruz. Opinions, findings, and conclusions are those of the authors and do not necessarily represent the views of the supporting organizations.

The manuscript benefited considerably from the comments of the Editor, Robin Williams, and reviewers and members of the Editorial Committee of the Rose Monograph Series.

x

1. Agriculture and the comparative analysis of production systems

The importance of agriculture as a production system is obvious. Agriculture constitutes a vital sector of production in *every* society, including ours. The fact, however, that agriculture is very much taken for granted in modern society is both interesting and unusual. With a production sector so important, why is so little public concern directed toward this segment of production?

One reason, of course, is that the urban way of life, particularly when reinforced by the complex division of labor, removes most people from the immediate *situs* of agricultural production. We live our lives thoroughly enmeshed in a division of labor in which agriculture leads a completely separated existence.

Popular journalism from time to time has helped to call attention to agriculture and rural life, especially during periods in which popular dissatisfaction with existing social arrangements has led to a "return to the land" in some fashion. During the hippie period of the 1960s, for example, considerable interest was manifested in small-scale agriculture. In the 1970s the interest in environmentalism led to concern about agriculture, particularly because it had become large in scale, monocultural, and chemical intensive. But except for the infrequent journalistic endeavors that illustrate some aspects of production, most people have little idea of the complex social paths – of the division of labor, the organization of production and distribution systems – necessary to deliver a head of iceberg lettuce to New York City or Wheeling, West Virginia, in January; nor, for that matter, how tomatoes become sauce delivered to the franchised pizza house in Minneapolis.

Agriculture is also taken for granted because it offers only limited employment opportunities. Although growth in employment has shifted to the professional and service sectors and manufacturing still involves tens of millions of people, agricultural employment has been steadily declining. The farm population reached its peak in 1916, declined slowly until 1945, and fell precipitously thereafter (Beale 1978, pp. 37–9). The

1

decline in farm population and employment was largely a function of the steady introduction of new technology that required larger and more capital-intensive units of production. At present, agriculture is so highly capitalized that less than 5 percent of the labor force produces most of the food required to feed the United States (Lerner 1975, Table D, pp. 11–25). At the same time, farm exports have increased.

However, agriculture, and its adjacent systems of organization, food processing, and preparation, are not simply complex technological systems: They are complex forms of a *social division of labor*. Why, then, is so little known or reported about the social organization of agricultural production or the social, political, and economic consequences of change in this sector?

At least part of the answer lies in the way in which two specific subdisciplines, rural sociology and agricultural economics, have exercised social science dominion over the agricultural sector. Our immediate concern is with rural sociology. Originally very much interested in agriculture, as the denudation of the rural sector reached epidemic proportions in the 1930s, rural sociologists moved away from agriculture and focused more intensively on rural community life. As rural communities disappeared, many rural sociologists moved their intellectual interests abroad, becoming expert about rural communities in the Philippines, Bolivia, and Pakistan rather than in the rural sections of New York, Wisconsin, or California. The process by which rural sociology became redirected away from agricultural production to other subjects and other geographical areas was complex but was a product of the very institutional enmeshing they experienced by being part of the land grant university system of the United States (Friedland 1979).

If careful analysis of the social organization of agricultural production did not develop within the knowledge-creating networks where it might have been expected, it also failed to appear within two wings of knowledge production – industrial sociology and Marxian labor process analysis – which might have functioned in this arena.

Industrial sociology set for itself the task of understanding social aspects of the division of labor within industrial organization. With its origins in the General Electric Hawthorne experiments conducted by Harvard faculty during the late 1920s and early 1930s (Roethlisberger and Dickson 1939; Mayo 1945; Sheppard 1949, 1950; Landsberger 1958; to cite only a portion of the literature), what began as a "human relations in industry" movement crystallized into industrial sociology after Wilbert Moore (1951) published an important synthesis of the field. During the remainder of the 1940s and through the 1950s industrial sociology developed an important body of literature that was largely (although not entirely) concerned with the loss of managerial control and the imperatives necessary to regain control that had been lost to workers during the upsurges of the 1930s (Burawoy 1979, Chapter 1).

Industrial sociology later splintered into several subfields: formal organization, which also was stimulated by Weber's work on complex social organization; the sociology of work; and occupations and professions. As if by definition, industrial sociology largely accepted the prevailing myth that work processes in *agriculture* were somehow different from industry. Two notable exceptions, Fisher (1953) and Stinchcombe (1961), explored the social organization of agricultural production; however, not until recently have others begun to elaborate on their work (e.g., Paige 1975; Thomas 1980a, b, c).

Neither industrial sociology nor the Marxists paid much attention to agriculture. Although the Communist Party had an interest in organizing blacks in the South and spent considerable energy in trying to understand southern agriculture, its analysis was, in fact, paralyzed by the imposition of a set of categories and orientations from outside. The examination of southern agriculture did not begin with an application of general Marxian categories about social relations; rather, it represented an a priori analysis created by an overall "vision" engendered in the Soviet Union.[1]

There was, perhaps, an even more profound impediment to the development of the analysis of agricultural production. Originating in classical Marxism, a tendency developed during the period of influence of the Second International to emphasize the trends within capitalism to increase the size and homogeneity of the working class. This theoretical blinder obscured the process of differentiation taking place *within* the working class, that is, the stratification of workers into status groups built around occupation, race, and sex. This was to become the critical distinction between the approach of mainstream sociology and Marxian social science. The former looked to "social stratification" with a basic set of assumptions about differentiation to explain differences in society; the latter, however, concentrated on social class with a primordial assumption about homogenization.

It took what might be characterized as a "semi-Marxist" comparative analysis to demonstrate that the differences in organization of the labor process produce economic stratification among occupations. Labor process organization will not *only* produce stratification but will also effect differing forms of consciousness corresponding to the economic strata within occupations. In this respect we consider Blauner's (1964) comparative analysis of four forms of work organization and Stinchcombe's (1959) essay on bureaucratic and craft administration of production to be important points of departure from the narrow foci of industrial sociology and earlier Marxian analysis. Their work set the foundation for the comparative analysis of production systems.

Although this study focuses on a single system of production, iceberg lettuce, we draw on comparative materials from a second agricultural commodity (tomatoes for processing) to demonstrate (1) similarities and differences in social and technical forms *within* the agricultural sector and (2) how these differences in production affect the composition of the labor force, the internal structure of firms, the external network of organizations relating to production, and the responses of participants (workers and capitalists) to their interaction in the production process.

The comparative analysis of production systems constitutes the broadest frame of reference for the present research. This study will draw from two bodies of theory: Marxian theories of the labor process and elements of industrial sociology/organization theory. This combination will be discussed at greater length in this chapter. However, the distinctions to be made between theories of the labor process and industrial sociology/organization theory are important and should be introduced early on.

The labor process is used to represent the organization of work activities and occupations *and* the relationships among social categories that are a result of those arrangements. Thus the capitalist labor process is characterized by the distinction between wage labor and owners/managers in the organization of work and by the production of value by labor and the appropriation of that value, in the form of unremunerated labor, by the capitalist. Industrial sociology and organization theory, although recognizing the potential for the opposed interests between workers and owners, generally discount the structural opposition of categories central to theories of the labor process; instead, their emphasis is on how organizations and their members work under various circumstances and in different environments. Although it would appear that these two bodies of theory might themselves be opposed, we will attempt to bring together the emphasis on problems of control and domination (labor process) with the problems of administration (industrial sociology/organization theory). Both schema, in our view, offer valuable insights into the study of stratification in industrial organizations.[2] Through the careful examination of specific production practices, we hope (1) to link the process of technological change to the social relationships found in production and (2) to illuminate the social differences that are produced by different labor processes.

The role of the state in agriculture

Implicit in the analysis of any production process is the role of the state. Because the state has consistently played a significant role in agricultural development, this issue is particularly pressing.

We do not intend here to present a complicated discussion of the character of the state, suffice it to note that we ourselves experience difficulties in dealing with instrumentalist notions of *the state* as "the executive committee of the bourgeoisie" or more pluralistic conceptions of "the government" (Miliband 1969; Dahl 1971). Although we believe the state to be something more complex than a social process engendered by the mode of production, it is difficult to delineate specifically the character of the state, partly because such a discussion tends to become reified as one is required to point to a particular entity like the government or a congeries of organizations.

We will attempt to illuminate state activity, in particular, as it is operationalized by and for agricultural interests. Although risking appearing functionalist in our approach, we begin by sketching in a discussion of the state, its character, and its role in agriculture. The analysis of state action offered here and later starts with the assumption that the state is constituted not only of the legislature and government administration that have created a network of formal legislation and organization but also in the interactions and processes with organized constituencies formed in and around agriculture. We see the state as being the process by which government and private entities meet and produce a network of legislation, administration, and knowledge production within the land grant science institutions to facilitate the process of capital accumulation within and adjacent to agriculture.

Therefore the state is conceived of as a central "figure." Historically, the intervention of the state has been notable in labor policy and scientific research. With respect to the agricultural labor market, this intervention has been relatively continuous for over a century. The state, for example, played a crucial role in providing the impetus for settlement and land improvement through legislation such as the Homestead Act. It later played a different role in the way in which western lands were "settled" to permit enormous landholdings, at least by comparison with the East and Midwest (McWilliams 1971, Chapter 2). The state played a vital role in removing labor from the land during the 1930s when technology could be utilized to substitute for labor. When labor came once again into short supply, the state (not simply the government, but the government in relation to organized groupings of growers) formulated a policy that provided an unlimited supply of labor to agriculture in the form of the *bracero* (see p. 145n1) program (Galarza 1964). When this policy came under criticism and was eliminated, the state permitted an effectively unrestricted flow of labor to agriculture and other industries, even while the government bemoaned its inability to close the border with Mexico.

In a very different way the state has organized one of the most complex scientific systems in the world to sustain agricultural production. This system has simultaneously facilitated the process of economic concentration and capital accumulation in agriculture. The U.S. Department of Agriculture (USDA) research network and the affiliated land grant universities have proven to be two of the most effective knowledge-producing institutions in the history of the development of science.[3]

This science system has been legitimated on the basis of the need to provide support to producers who are too small to develop the scientific knowledge themselves. Yet the system, with distinctive value orientations and commitments built into it and socialized into its personnel, has developed to the point where its integration with big agriculture and large-scale agri-industrial enterprises is thorough and unquestioned.

Agriculture and the capitalist mode of production

Agriculture is composed of a complex of specialized production systems. The peculiarities of weather and soil in the making of food and fiber crops should not, however, obscure the universal character of commodity production in capitalist agriculture. We will undertake an analysis of the social organization of lettuce production in identical fashion as, for example, the making of automobiles. Following Marx, we want to consider agricultural production in the United States, and in capitalist societies more generally, as simply one distinct segment of the *capitalist mode of production*. The capitalist mode of production means that productive forms are assembled for the purpose of making profit. Family farming, corporate farming, and the various admixtures found in the United States, are primarily concerned with the production of commodities that will be moved into exchange for profit. Profit, in turn, will be largely reinvested in the development of more means of production.

The two basic components of the mode of production are the means of production and the social relations of production. The means of production constitute all the elements necessary to develop a productive system. In the case of agriculture this involves particularly *land*. However, it also involves a host of auxiliary elements that we normally associate with the term "technology" but which can be designated by the more common-sensical notion of tools.

The shaping of the means of production is, in turn, very substantially a function of the *social relations of production*. This term encompasses the social relationships that are constructed in the process of producing any constellation of commodities within a mode of production. Thus, at a very elemental level, the social relations of agricultural production today, in the United States, are very different from what they were in 1860, for example, when the mode of production within agriculture was characterized by several different forms, including capitalist production (particularly in the Northeast), slavery (in the South), and subsistence (in the far Midwest).

The "family farm," for example, is a specific organizational form within the capitalist mode of production. But this organization constitutes only part of the totality of social relationships. If a farmer and his or her spouse produce many offspring to participate in production, the relationships with their children become encompassed in the social relations of production. Similarly, if a farmer hires a year-round employee – a "hired hand" – this constitutes a different social relationship. If the farmer employs seasonal workers at harvest for three-week periods, we are discussing still different social relationships.

If the term "social relations of production" encompasses a number of relationships, these *all* stand in contrast to the kinds of social relations encountered in different modes of production. For example, in slave systems, the social relations of production are limited by virtue of the fact that the laborer is himself or herself property. This produces different forms of organization of production because, among other things, the owner must deal with the slave in periods when the slave becomes unproductive, for example, through advanced age, whereas in capitalism this is not the case, for the costs are either borne by the unemployed worker or are thrown on to society through the welfare system.

This brief introduction is intended only to set the stage for the more concrete analysis of the social organization of agriculture. Of necessity, it emphasizes the productive process rather than the derivative social processes, thereby highlighting the differences in emphasis between a sociology of agriculture – and concomitantly the comparative analysis of production systems – and rural sociology. The fact the rural society was once associated with agriculture has decreasing relevance. Unquestionably the origins of the two, agriculture and rural society, were the same. When rural sociology named itself and focused on social organization and proceeded to exclude the productive process from serious consideration it brought about its own demise.[4]

On the labor process

Through comparisons of the lettuce industry with other agricultural and nonagricultural production systems, we will argue that fundamental similarities prevail in the structure of social and economic organizations in agricultural and nonagricultural sectors. Of equal importance is the analysis of the factors that influence the organization of production in capitalist industries: How are new methods of production formulated? What forces determine the acceptance or rejection of new technologies? Translated into questions related to our case study: What factors led to the development of a mechanical lettuce harvester? What conditions will lead to its introduction? What consequences might be expected as a result of the mechanization of harvesting?

In order to analyze the problem of change in the organization of agricultural production, we will focus on the labor process. The labor process is conceived not simply as the *physical* organization of work but as the *meeting ground* of the two major social categories: wage labor and capital. In the labor process these social categories shape one another through dynamic and structured interaction; that is, they make one another in the process of producing commodities or things. The relationship between workers and owners/managers pivots on the production of value by one category (labor) and the appropriation of that value by the other category (capital).

The development of the capitalist form of production and the social relationships attendant to it is contingent on its ability simultaneously to accomplish two purposes: (1) to convert labor into a commodity to be hired in the service of capital and (2) to secure the consent of the bearers of this commodity – workers – to participate in the inequality relationship. That is, the critical factors for capitalist economic organizations are labor supply and labor control. Regarding the first purpose, the subordination of independent producers to capitalist manufacture was accomplished historically through the "freeing" of peasant labor from servitude, on the one hand, and the destruction of independent craft production, on the other. Activities once circumscribed by the lord–peasant relationship or performed independently were subsumed by the division of labor between and within capitalist enterprises. Stripped of the means by which to exist independent of capital, workers must choose among participation, opposition, or starvation.

The intensification of labor in ever more productive forms of manufacture has been accomplished through the subordination and division of craft activity to the industrial division of labor. This process, nevertheless, remains contingent on the willingness of laborers to participate in the wage-labor contract. The second purpose of capitalist production, therefore, involves the problem of domination, that is, the process of organizing the consent of subordinate categories, in this case, workers, to accept existing arrangements. If workers stand opposed to the de-skilling of their crafts or to the intensification of the activities they perform, they simultaneously threaten the existence of the opposing category in the relationship – the capitalists:

When (the capitalist) buys labor time, the outcome is far from being either so certain or so definite that it can be reckoned with precision and in advance. This is merely an expression of the fact that the portion of his capital expended on labor power is the "variable" portion, which undergoes an increase in the process of production; for him the question is how great that increase will be. It thus becomes essential for the capitalist that control over the labor process pass from the hands of the worker into his own. This transition presents itself in history as the progressive *alienation of the process of production* from the worker; to the capitalist, it presents itself as the problem of *management* (Braverman 1974, pp. 57–8).

The subjective elements in the development and intensification of the capitalist labor process were of signal importance to Karl Marx and his successors. The intensification of the class struggle, they argued, would result from the homogenization of the conditions of the working class and the intensification of capitalist exploitation. This would result in an end in which the opposition inherent in the structural relationship between workers and capitalists would emerge as conscious warfare between classes.

Although the capitalist system and capitalist enterprises have demonstrated remarkable capacity to absorb, ameliorate, and/or displace class struggle, conflict has not been stifled entirely. Yet great attention has been paid by social scientists to those instances of labor–capital struggle that have taken a highly visible form: strikes, labor legislation, and the formation of worker-based economic and political movements. Only in recent years have Marxist and neo-Marxist social scientists recaptured Marx's original intense concern with the organization and development of the capitalist labor process. Studies by Braverman (1974), Burawoy (1979), Marglin (1974), Kraft (1977), and Noble (1978), among others, have reintroduced the labor process as a critical area for study.

Burawoy and Noble, in particular, make problematic the issue of cooperation between workers and capitalists in an effort to examine the development and implementation of the labor process. Burawoy argues, in part, that the consent of labor to participate in the inequality relationship is the product of the struggle on the shop floor. The organization of the labor process is itself an object of political as well as economic struggle (Burawoy 1979, Chapter 10). Conflicts in Burawoy's machine shop between machine operators and managers over rates and job specifications constitute part of the less visible class struggle. Struggle over the shape and terms of the labor process, Burawoy suggests, consists of, but is not restricted to, "rate setting" or "soldiering" on the shop floor. Rather, the effort to restrict the "detailing" of work and to wrest some degree of control over work activities is a continuous process in the capitalist enterprise. The capacity to absorb or ameliorate those conflicts constitutes the game that serves to generate consent among workers. Burawoy's analysis further reveals that the design and implementation of new work processes are also objects of struggle.

Noble's (1978) contribution to the analysis of the labor process concerns precisely this last aspect: the forces influencing the physical and social organization of production. The configuration of computer-controlled machining, Noble suggests, is not the end product of some inevitable or unidirectional technological flow; Noble rejects technological determinist arguments. Rather, technological development is tempered by real and potential struggle on the part of workers. Noble's study demonstrates that considerable attention is paid by both engineers and managers to anticipating how workers might undermine or retard their control over the labor process. Management's failure to produce a "conflict-free" labor process, in turn, substantiates Burawoy's thesis.

In our own study close attention will be paid to the organization of the labor process in agricultural production, especially within the lettuce industry. The questions that Burawoy and Noble use to study the labor process will be fundamental to the study of past and potential changes in lettuce production. We will, however, seek to enlarge the scope of the analysis in an effort to incorporate specific labor processes and activities connected to lettuce harvesting. That is, rather than confine the research to harvesting alone, we will examine conditions in related work such as preharvest operations, handling, and transportation to consider how they affect the harvest labor process. Furthermore, we will incorporate political, economic, and social factors external but directly related, to lettuce harvesting. In this context we refer both to controls afforded agricultural producers by the availability of noncitizen labor, documented and undocumented, and the increasing unionization of lettuce workers. The issue of documentation of workers – having legal status as contrasted to being without proper documents – is significant in that it affects the capability of such workers to insist on their rights and their ability to organize.

The expansion of the scope of the study beyond the confines of a particular firm or shop limits the specificity of the argument. However, by broadening the unit of analysis to a crop-industry we believe we may incorporate greater variety and experience. The industry-as-unit further meshes with our effort to promote a methodology for the comparative analysis of production systems.

In summary, considerable emphasis has been given and will continue to be placed throughout this study on the organization of the labor process. In explaining the preconditions and extent of technological change in the organization of production, we are suggesting that the interrelated factors of labor supply and labor control operate as important independent variables. That is, we focus on the labor process because it is both the fundamental structural meeting ground of the major social categories and because the specific underpinnings of the capitalist mode of production provide the parameters for technological innovation and change. Bolstering the theoretical importance of this model is the historical centrality of labor supply and labor control in the organization of U.S. agriculture. As will be described, one of the major differences in technological sophistication between manufacturing and agriculture has been the *nonproblematic* character of agricultural labor supply and control.

Operationalizing a model for a sociology of agriculture

Before we address more specifically the operationalization of a sociology of agriculture, it will be useful to make two methodological points. Choosing the appropriate unit of analysis has an important bearing on the conduct of research. As outlined earlier, the analysis of lettuce production in this study uses the crop or commodity as its focus. Deciding where to make the break between what is and what is not to be included is partially determined by the research problem: that is, we consciously choose to focus on those factors directly related to the production of lettuce. Rural sociologists will note, for example, that the concept of community does not appear as an integral part of the analysis.[5]

Because we conceive of an analytic separation between industrial agriculture and rural communities, these communities are assumed to have little measurable effect on the organization of agricultural production. If anything, the influence travels in the opposite direction. Perhaps we are willing to err in the direction of overly stressing the labor process in economic organization to avoid the pitfalls of past community research under rural sociological influences.[6]

A second unit of analysis is subsumed by our focus on the crop-industry or commodity: the firm or the unit of production. Our approach focuses on the commodity as the crucial unit of analysis. Of necessity, this approach emphasizes certain kinds of phenomena for explanation and deemphasizes others. One consequence, in the present study, is that the *farm* as a unit of analysis is very much ignored. The unavailability (or lack thereof) of data and/or the limitations of time and resources to conduct additional research is the reason for this rather than the inherent logic of our methodology. An alternative approach to the analysis of agriculture might focus on class structure around which production is organized.

Although our data are not directly drawn from case studies of individual firms, the sociological problem we confront, the determinants of change in the agricultural labor process, makes us sensitive to trends and differences in the organization of producing firms. We will thus introduce differences in organizational approaches *between* firms carrying on the same activities (e.g., growing, shipping, brokeraging, etc.) and firms carrying on different activities (e.g., growing and shipping versus growing). At this point, the availability of data lead us to a stronger focus on the industry rather than on the firm.

More data are collected and made public about commodities than about the firms producing them largely as a result of two factors: (1) the rather limited information (both public and private) about earnings, corporate structure, and management of individual firms in the agricultural sector and (2) the structure of firm ownership, where firms are mostly either closely held corporations or subsidiary corporations. In the first instance, little if anything gets reported beyond the relatively small core of shareholders. Thus we will provide some information on one lettuce firm when it proposed to "go public." When this firm dropped the idea, no further internal information became available. In the second case,

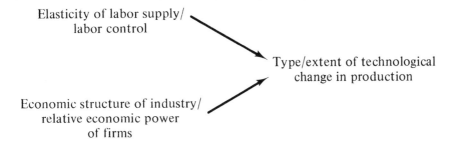

Figure 1.1   Simple causal model of technological change

little information other than gross earnings and expenditure figures are available through annual reports (e.g., the annual report of United Brands for its subsidiary Sun Harvest) or the 10-K reports required by the Securities and Exchange Commission.

More importantly, we will suggest that the economic organization of an industry, as well as the labor supply/control variable, will have an independent effect on the range of choices or options for technological change in production. The relative economic power or market strength of the major categories of firms in an industry will have a distinct influence on our dependent variable of technological change. As will be demonstrated in the lettuce industry discussions (Chapters 3 and 4) and the summary of the processing tomato industry (Chapter 2), the strategies of firms toward technological change will be greatly affected by their relative positions in their industries.

Within the context of the empirical case study of lettuce, Figure 1.1 depicts in simplified form the basic causal model with which we will begin our explanation of technological change. We will elaborate on this model and modify it in the following chapters and will conclude with an assessment of its utility in explaining the lettuce and tomato case studies in the final chapter. Our approach to the sociology of agriculture is shown schematically in Figure 1.2.

A sociology of agriculture should be concerned with the entire production, processing, and distribution system, not simply with the *growing* of a commodity. The storage, treatment, processing, transportation, marketing, promotion, and sales are all part of the system of analysis. For practicality, it may not be feasible to analyze every aspect. However, if

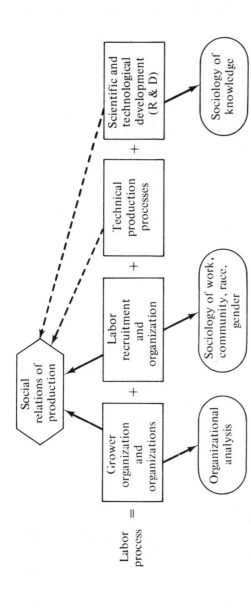

Figure 1.2   Model for a sociology of agriculture: processes and bodies of knowledge

we consider what has happened in agricultural production over the past century, we can note how the different elements of systemic production have been differentiated out of, and away from, agriculture. Originally, farming was largely a self-sufficient activity in which the farmer produced not only the crop but the tools necessary to produce the crop and the storage and processing facilities as well.

As capitalist industrial production expanded, activities once conducted as part of a single, integrated system of production – the farm – were differentiated away from it to the city and the factory. Tool production, for example, stopped on the farm when tools such as ploughs and hoes could be produced more efficiently by blacksmiths and in factories. Farming became a constrained activity. This development was accelerated when construction of the scientific network of the land grant system began, emphasizing specialization of activity. Seed production was removed from the actual producer to specialized producers. Processing of crops moved out of the hands of farmers to those of canners. Storage was centralized with specialists who bought, sold, and stored commodities (Rasmussen 1960; Braverman 1974; Mandel 1975). The differentiation process is represented schematically in Figure 1.3.

Much of what once would have been incorporated into a sociology of agriculture is now very distant from it. Thus there is little point in including the production of tractors, farm machinery, and farm implements into a sociology of agriculture. Although this technical means of production undoubtedly plays a role, we can essentially omit it from our analytic scheme. In contrast, the analysis of another technical means of production, the machinery, tools, equipment, and their usage in agricultural preparation, production, and processing, plays an important part in the development of a sociology of agriculture.

Perhaps the best way to begin the specifications of a sociology of agriculture is to delineate the basic elements that are set out in Figure 1.2.

Grower organization and organizations

We begin with growers because they are the major formative element of agricultural production. Akin to the manufacturer, industrialist, or employer in industry, the grower is the basic agent shaping the productive process. Production is delineated not exclusively by the action of growers; as will be argued, there is an interaction among the various factors that constitute the labor process that determine the character of agricultural production. However, the grower constitutes the beginning point.

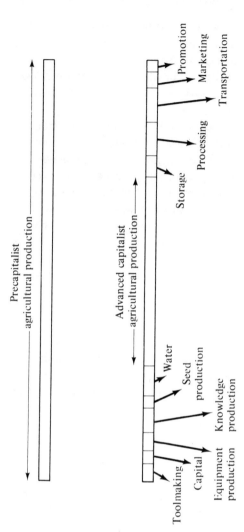

Figure 1.3   Labor process differentiation in capitalist agriculture

The emphasis given here to the grower as a starting point stresses the interaction of growers – as employers and as capitalists – with workers. Also, growers are the focus of a variety of forces involved in agricultural production. These forces include market factors, credit restrictions and availabilities, production requirements, and so on. While emphasizing the interaction of growers with labor, we are not simply ignoring these other factors but are unable to deal with all of them in the space allowed.

Each grower of each commodity or combination of commodities organizes production in distinct ways, although there are some important differences in how production is organized, dependent on the size of the enterprise. At the simplest level, annual crops require very different forms of organization from crops that are to be produced over many years. A grower of lettuce in California or of wheat in North Dakota must organize production significantly differently from a grower of cherries in Michigan or of oranges in Florida.

The growing of distinctive commodities or groups of commodities is usually shaped in a limited number of patterns. For example, there are a limited number of ways in which producers can organize to "manufacture green gold," although there are numerous variations in practice within those basic patterns. These patterns will stand in sharp contrast to the patterns found in the production of other agricultural commodities, for example, processing tomatoes. Because tomatoes are produced exclusively for processing and lettuce effectively has no way of being processed, the organization of production in the two annual crops is very different. Lettuce producers tend to be more complex in their organization because they must deliver a crop of unusual delicacy to a great many geographically dispersed markets fifty-two weeks a year. Tomato production, in contrast, is much simpler despite tendencies toward concentration, which have led to increased size of production units and therefore increased complexity.

Each producing unit (grower) develops some pattern of production, but growers, as a constellation, create *organizations*. The forms these organizations take and their capacity to function vis-à-vis other organizations in the production and distribution system all constitute another subject for analysis.[7] The forms of commodity-specific organization can be manifold but generally fall into four major types: production research (such as plant breeding, disease research, and cultivaton and harvesting technology), advertising and marketing, political action and legislative lobbying, and labor relations (including labor recruitment and contract negotiations).[8]

The network of organizations is not limited to specific commodities.

Surrounding them there are a network of geographically based, multi-purpose organizations (the Farm Bureau Federation, National Grange, National Farmers Union, National Farmers Organization, etc.); geographically based single-purpose organizations such as producer co-ops; functionally based associations such as the National Council of Agricultural Employers or the National Cotton Council, which keep their eyes on legislation; and special-purpose organizations created for particular activities.

Labor recruitment and organization

No production gets done exclusively by a farmer nor, indeed, has it ever been done in this way. Even in the relatively simpler productive systems of earlier times, the farm wife was an essential part of production as well as of biological and social *reproduction*. The issue of gender thus immediately impinges on any analysis of the organization of labor as a factor of production. How labor gets recruited to the production process and how it is organized constitutes the second major problem of a sociology of agriculture. When agricultural production was simple, this process was enmeshed and undifferentiated from family organization. Nowadays, it is clear that a more complex analysis of labor recruitment and organization is necessary.

Whether workers are employed on a year-round basis, seasonally, for wages on an hourly basis or on piecework, for exchange, and the like, constitutes the analysis of labor within a sociology of agriculture. Here we note that although rural sociology has not dealt with these issues very effectively, economics has been far more successful.

In many cases how labor is recruited and organized depends not only on grower organizaion but on the technical practices involved and the way in which the crop must be handled. Wheat, for example, can be harvested by specialized contractors who recruit their own crews. This system would not do in strawberries in central California where there is a long season and the requirements of constant attention to the beds gives rise to what is called "share farming" but is, in fact, an unusual system of employing workers and their families for one-year cycles while maintaining a piecework system. Similarly, lettuce harvesting is done by specialists who travel with the crop but who are very unlike the migrants found in soft fruits in Michigan or New York. Also, the recruitment and organization of workers in egg factories is greatly different from that found in sheep production.

Any examination of the labor factor inevitably involves, then, an analysis not only of communities, because it is from communities that labor is often drawn, but of race, ethnicity, and gender. The fact that there is a racial–ethnic division of labor in complex large-scale production, for example, is hardly accidental. Similarly, the fact that women are employed in some forms of production but not others, for example, wrapped-lettuce harvest but not naked-lettuce harvest, demands examination.

Another subject that falls within the purview of this analysis is the character of interaction that occurs between capitalist and worker, between the grower and those who work for the grower. Activities of *conflict and struggle* have taken different form in agriculture from that elsewhere. Despite a great many attempts of workers to organize themselves, two factors have combined to create obstacles to farm worker organization: (1) the isolated and differentiated character of production (Morin 1952) and (2) the awesome political power of agricultural employers. The differences within agriculture are not unique, however; similarities exist, in a structural sense, in office work and retail sales, for example.

Two distinct questions are, therefore, germane to this subject: (1) What have been the differences between agriculture and other production systems that have led to very different outcomes from those in industry? (2) What forms of struggle exist now and have been manifested historically?

Forms of struggle do not only take the form of *organizing unions*. Unionization is the most obvious and dramatic form of struggle, but it also represents a form of accommodation. Understanding the character of struggle requires, therefore, close analysis of daily interaction between farmer and worker. In carrying out this part of the analysis, we will draw on the work of Burawoy (1979) and Noble (1978). Furthermore, it is in the interaction between this factor (labor–management conflict) and grower/industry organization that we find the emergence of the social relations of production.

Labor is not simply a quiescent factor to be organized passively by grower employers; it is a factor that is constantly interactive, whereby the relations of production are worked out concretely and specifically. These relations can be variable. For example, lettuce harvesting requires a skilled and experienced labor force available to move with the crop. Soft fruit production, in contrast, has a season that may last three weeks. Thus the demand for and treatment of labor will be very different as between fruit and lettuce production. Relations of production, in other words, are continually being developed through the interaction between growers and their workers. This interaction obviously also includes the problem of recruitment of workers.

The social relations of production are not limited to these two factors because, as we will argue, the development of science (e.g., specific bodies of knowledge, as well as the formulation of technical production practices) is often concerned with reducing uncertainty in production. Some of these uncertainties are labor induced and scientists and technologists are therefore drawn into developing technical practices aimed at creating better control over the labor factor.

Technical production practices

A sociology of agriculture must pay attention to technical production practices. These involve the way in which production itself is organized. As will be discussed later on, we will find that commanding bodies of data about the technical practices of production constitutes a difficult, but necessary, task in understanding a commodity production system. The technical practices in growing processing tomatoes, for example, involve close scheduling to encompass temperature factors, the rate of growth, *and delivery dates.* In performing their work, scientists and technologists have discovered that tomato production can be scheduled. This leads to the adoption of a number of technical practices that not only include the irrigation schedule, which affects how labor is immediately utilized and how new harvest workers will be recruited and organized, but also the application of chemical regulators. All these factors impinge on the demand for and the utilization of labor; therefore it is necessary to know a considerable amount about technical production processes.

Scientific and technological development

The organization of the production of scientific and technological information constitutes the final focus that must be considered in the development of a sociology of agriculture.

What is notable about agriculture, similar to industry, is that it is now a highly technical and complex production process based on very high levels of scientific knowledge and information distribution. It is also different from industry in that the bulk of scientific and technological development (R&D) has occurred in the public sector, for example, in the land grant system of colleges and universities and in the U.S. Department of Agriculture. Although much R&D occurs in the private sector, the bulk of R&D relating to agriculture continues to be publicly funded. In this respect, agriculture occupies an "exceptional" position in contrast to how R&D has been conducted in other production sectors.

As in other sectors, a fundamental characteristic of the R&D system has been its concentration on reducing uncertainty and increasing productivity. These two correlated goals have given the R&D network within American agriculture its distinctive characteristics. Generally, R&D has contributed to the concentration of agricultural production, the entry into production of corporate enterprises through vertical integration, and the development of the incorporated family-based production unit. R&D, in other words, has had the consequence of producing concentration because it has fitted the process of capital formation in agriculture, capital growth, and capital transfer into nonagricultural sectors. All these elements constitute that vital process of capital accumulation that Marx regarded as an essential feature of capitalism. In this respect the R&D network has contributed to the transformation of agriculture from small-scale production to forms characteristic of the more general system of capitalist production, for example, large-scale, concentrated, highly oriented toward profit maximization, and reinvestment.[9]

A central problem in the consideration of the R&D network utilizing a commodity focus rests on the way the body of knowledge with respect to a given commodity develops. Bodies of knowledge, for example, do not descend from either the sky or the isolated brains of scholars, each producing his or her great thoughts and concerned about protecting their academic freedom. Rather, bodies of knowledge emerge from the constant interaction of differential forces involved in the labor process.

Thus, to take a somewhat familiar example, the body of knowledge in processing tomato production is not generalized over every potential aspect of production. In fact, a goodly portion of the body of knowledge is related to (1) control over the labor factor and (2) the maintenance of delivery (production) schedules. Research on new tomato varieties, which have proliferated since the early 1960s, is concerned with the development of a tomato that will harvest better by machine. These researches have been ramified to fit the differential requirements of different districts and therefore different geophysical conditions to fit the needs of the processors for a regular supply over an extended period of time. Similarly, research on handling of lettuce after harvest has been concentrated on incremental changes that will save labor, on a transformational change to reduce labor requirements, and on more effective ways to deliver lettuce at distant markets with reduced spoilage (Hinsch and Rij 1976; Hinsch et al. 1976).

Some topics are clearly designated as important in land grant R&D; however, other topics are clearly unimportant. Thus a tomato vine was designed for mechanical harvesting. This led to the development of a vine that would produce a lot of flowers simultaneously (to produce a heavy set) and a lot of tomatoes that would all mature at the same time. This also required the development of a plant with a very heavy central stalk to support the weight of the tomatoes. Although this sort of vine was designed, another sort of vine was *not* designed, for example, a vine that would begin to produce flowers early in the season and which would produce tomatoes on a continuing basis for a long time. This latter vine might be described as a "labor vine," one which would produce maximum potential earnings to workers over an extended period. The fact that a "machine vine" was designed and not a "labor vine" is not accidental. Thus the shaping of the body of scientific and technological knowledge in different commodities constituted an important arena in the sociology of knowledge.

Conclusion

The framework of Marxian analysis has led us to direct the sociology of agriculture toward conceptualizing the totality of the production system. That is, agriculture must be conceptualized as a system of social organization that includes, among other factors, production and exchange. We contend that it is possible to develop an analysis of agriculture as an overall social system and simultaneously develop a systematic frame of reference for comparing agricultural production to other systems of production.

2. Theory and method

This chapter considers several theoretical and methodological issues central to the examination of lettuce production and to the projection of the social consequences of harvest mechanization, which will be examined in the next two chapters. Because labor, as a factor, represents a crucial element in the transition to mechanized harvesting, several theoretical formulations about the character of labor markets will be examined initially. We begin with a classical theoretical statement on the character of agricultural labor markets and then turn to a more general theoretical formulation concerning internal labor markets within employing organizations.

Second, because this study sets out to specify the conditions under which the transition to mechanized lettuce harvesting will occur and the social consequences that will derive, we now consider the methodology that will be employed. By indicating the conceptual approaches taken, we intend not only to open the process we employ to scrutiny and criticism but to suggest the capability of systematic application of similar procedures in other studies.

Because our methodology heavily stresses the importance of comparative analysis, the chapter will conclude with a summary of a case study of processing tomatoes completed earlier. Our intention in including the case study here is twofold. First, the tomato study not only came before the lettuce analysis but, in fact, illuminated the latter. Many of the conceptual, methodological, and definitional procedures followed were developed through the research on the social organization of tomato production. Second, and more important, the tomato summary will be used explicitly throughout the present analysis. Although we will use tomato data only briefly in the two chapters that follow, the final chapter will draw systematically and comparatively on materials from the two studies as we develop formulations relevant not only for a sociology of agriculture but for the comparative analysis of production systems.

Comparative labor market analysis

Lloyd Fisher's study, *The Harvest Labor Market in California* (1953), constitutes one of the best theoretical analyses of the organization of the labor market in agriculture. Fisher contended that although the harvest labor market was changing and would be further changed by mechanization, the fundamental characteristics of the labor market were determined by California's "specialization in labor-intensive crops, and the intense seasonal demand for labor which results" (Fisher 1953, p. 2). To resolve this problem, Fisher described the labor market as being "structureless" and having five characteristics (Fisher 1953, pp. 7–9):

There are no unions setting conditions for job entry and exit.

There are impersonal relations between employer and employee.

Jobs are unskilled and accessible to a large and unspecialized labor force.

Compensation is by unit produced rather than by time.

Operations must employ little or no capital in machinery.

The crucial problem for growers, therefore, becomes one of labor supply: Labor must be continually available. Fisher sees the consequent "flooding" of the labor market less as a function of keeping wages low (although this consequence, it will be seen, is important for growers) but more as being related to the character of harvest activities and the conditions under which the labor supply is produced:

The farmer's demand is more or less as he states it. He can, by and large, provide some employment for most of the workers he calls for. He could also harvest his crop with many less. So long as the cost of recruiting additional labor remains negligible and the cost of unemployment is borne by the community, and so long as the piece rate prevails, the farmer will continue to demand a larger number of workers for a shorter period of time in preference to a smaller number of workers for a longer period of time (Fisher 1953, p. 11).

The agricultural labor market, unlike the industrial labor market, therefore, is maintained as readily accessible, according to Fisher, by being "subject to substantial expansions of supply from at least four sources . . . " These include (Fisher 1953, pp. 15–16):

Surplus labor from the city in periods of depression and unemployment.

A constant stream of migrants to the Pacific Coast.

Mobilization of labor from rural towns.

The organized importation of labor by the federal government.

The fourth source was organized, at the time Fisher wrote, as the *bracero*[1] program. This program ended formally in 1964. Despite this, the harvest labor system continues to be geared to creation of an oversupply of workers in a relatively unstructured labor market to ensure that enough harvest workers are available at the peak of demand.

Fisher's analysis of the unstructured labor market in agriculture, published in 1953, is somewhat obsolete, especially because a number of structural changes have occurred in agricultural production and the organization of the labor market. Since that time there have also been several important theoretical formulations about the labor market, even though in conditions and circumstances different from those in agriculture, but with bearing on this subject. Therefore, it will be useful to examine the agricultural labor market in terms of the analyses developed in recent years of both "dual labor markets" and "external" and "internal" labor markets (Doeringer and Piore 1971; Burawoy 1979). An external labor market refers to what was traditionally known as *the* labor market – a system for the allocation of individuals to jobs in employment. An internal labor market is "an administrative unit, such as a manufacturing plant, within which the pricing and allocation of labor is governed by a set of administrative rules and procedures" (Doeringer and Piore 1971, pp. 1–2). As Burawoy (1979) notes, sociologists have long known about the existence of the internal labor market through organizational analysis and the study of bureaucracies. But the concept of the internal labor market, as Burawoy notes, is useful for sociologists "in sensitizing one to the linkage between internal and external changes in the emergence of the modern firm" (Burawoy 1979, p. 96). Application of these concepts to lettuce production will demonstrate the commonalities between lettuce production organizations and other industrial organizations.

Initially, in the type of labor market described by Fisher there is no internal labor market; what internal labor market exists is masked by family organization. As agricultural production becomes more complex and integrated, a labor force is required beyond the family. Two factors produce an internal labor force: (1) the sheer size of organization increases and (2) the division of labor increases and becomes more complex. As production organizations increase in size and complexity, the need for the establishment of rules becomes necessary. Differences in skill levels emerge as an important differentiating mechanism, with which develop some regularized, objectified procedures for moving between jobs that open prospects for job mobility within the organization.

The forms of production organization in California agriculture have changed substantially since Fisher conducted his analysis in 1953. Not only did the bracero program, with its capacity to supply as much labor as necessary, come to an end but other more profound structural changes occurred in agriculture, particularly in lettuce production. The development of a new technology for cooling lettuce permitted a shift in the organization of production. The new technology undermined the ability of unions of packingshed workers to exercise some degree of control over working conditions (Glass 1966). The resultant reorganization of the labor process and the labor market created the preconditions for the internalization of segments of the lettuce labor force.

The significant theoretical points to be emphasized, however, are:

1. Labor market analysis constitutes a vital consideration in the examination of any given agricultural production system. The labor supply represents a major problem, as Fisher pointed out, and should not be taken for granted.
2. Production systems and their organization are continually evolving, as are the conditions affecting the labor market. No theoretical formulation, therefore, is useful forever but must undergo constant modification. The applications of the theoretical formulations with respect to the labor market will be clarified in Chapter 3.

Conceptual problems and dilemmas of social projection

This study undertakes an analysis of the conditions under which technological change will take place in the lettuce industry. On the basis of an examination of the social organization of the industry, we intend to project a set of possible social consequences with varying degrees of likelihood.

It is important, however, that we be conceptually clear at the outset in distinguishing between two related, but different concepts: *prediction* and *projection*. In earlier work (Friedland 1974; Friedland and Barton 1975) the terms "prediction" and "predictive methodology" were utilized (1) to distinguish the object of our efforts from the post-factum assessment of technological change and (2) to alert readers to the need to develop a set of research methods for the performance of such studies. Reviewing the literature since that time, as well as through the comments of colleagues, we have become aware that the use of the term "prediction" is at variance with the manner in which it is used by quantitative analysts, particularly systems analysts and econometricians. To this group of researchers, prediction involves the construction of mathematical models and the as-

signment of confidence intervals to statements about relationships between measured and/or ranked variables. Currently, such research
methodology represents a set of procedures to which we make no pre-
tense of being engaged. The term "projection" has, therefore, been sub-
stituted to avoid creating confusion.

It should be noted, however, that the change in terminology in no way
reflects a lessening of importance attached to the research findings nor
should it detract from the rigor of the method we have undertaken to
follow. First, we are concerned with the production of knowledge about
the relationships among social groups as they interact with one another.
Inasmuch as the research subject with which this study is concerned has
not been scrutinized closely in the past, much of what is being done here
lies beyond the boundaries of an established body of literature. As a
result, this study must rely on "hard" data somewhat less than similar
studies do. The data used, for example, include interviews with knowl-
edgeable participants in the industry, in all production categories, but not
structured survey schedules or sophisticated manipulation of census information. This methodology does not preclude the analysis of such data;
however, at this point, given the state of data sources, we have found
such sophisticated practices unproductive and have focused on an understanding of the character and history of relationships between actors,
both human and organizational, in the industry. Although not involving
ourselves in extensive quantitative analysis at this juncture, we consider
our research activities as prefatory and necessary to their later conduct.

Second, although recognizing the tentative nature of the projections
made, especially when compared to some degree of statistical confidence,
we would note that the methodology utilized has the advantage of captur-
ing the process of social change. We assume that the lettuce industry, for
example, is undergoing change and so we are forced to be sensitive to the
fluid character of relationships between groups, although not suggesting
that relationships are amorphous and therefore unmeasurable. Rather,
we assert that the relationships are structural and systematic. But, in
contrast to the models often developed by econometricians and others,
this study is more concerned with creating a range of projections about
future events than with highly restricted "point estimates."

Third, our projections must be distinguished from statistically derived
projections through the status accorded relationships between the categories or variables. As Schnaiberg and Meidinger (1978) and others have
suggested, one of the major weaknesses of statistical modeling resides in
its unquestioning emphasis on the relationships between variables. That

is, the existence of statistically significant relationships between variables overrides the theoretical explanation of the relationship itself. A model is admired for its mathematical elegance or sophistication, not for its explanatory power. In this sense we depart considerably from the formulation of projections. The intent of the present study is to make the existence of such relationships problematic in order that we do not reinforce the acceptance of elegant but unquestioned explanations.

As we consider the need and the potential utility of projective analyses, we find that the type of endeavor represented by the present study is rarely undertaken within the agricultural sciences. Even though there exists in the United States an enormous research and development apparatus known as the state agricultural experiment stations and the cooperative extension services, integrated and coordinated through the U.S. Department of Agriculture, the connection between the social sciences and agriculture is only weakly developed through this apparatus (Hathaway 1972). Although an enormous amount of exploratory research and development is carried on, relatively little exploration is conducted in the social sciences. And what little research is conducted is concentrated in agricultural economics, most particularly in production and mobility analyses. Thus the exploration undertaken through the present study must be based less on past sociological findings within agriculture and must utilize studies conducted elsewhere, in nonagricultural settings.

Beyond this problem, however, lie other even more significant ones. Human beings are not, like other animals, simply *re*active entities; they are symbolizing and interpreting creatures who internalize values and attitudes and respond to their changing environments. Humans plan but their plans are often sent askew by "unanticipated consequences" (Merton 1936; Selznick 1953), which are the result of individuals and groups interpreting events and utilizing them for their own interests and purposes. The reactive character of human beings and human groups makes the process of social projection especially hazardous. One possible solution to reactivity would be to make social projections and then withhold them from scrutiny until a specified period of time has transpired. This process, however, would not only delay the development of a projective methodology but could be open to a variety of abuses. Despite the uncertainties created by reactivity of humans, we believe it advantageous to undertake the risks involved to facilitate the development of projective methodology.

We can note still another problem in undertaking social projection. Social scientists, by their very training, are traditionally reluctant to venture into projective analysis. Our training gears us more toward historical and current analyses rather than toward projections. We know from experience that the study of the past and the present can lead to considerable controversy and debate. Why undertake anything as dubious as ventures into the future? The tools of social science, it has been argued, are sufficiently weak to require that our endeavors be more modest.

This reluctance is further exacerbated as a result of the special history of the social sciences as related to agriculture. Rather than constituting an important and vital aspect of agricultural research, the two most relevant bodies, economics and sociology, have been only weakly developed, and along very limited lines. Rural sociology, for example, is singularly unenlightening as a discipline concerned with the character and condition of rural society. It reports a little about the social characteristics of farmers and the social organization of the rural community but *very* little about the labor process in agriculture (Stokes and Miller 1975; Friedland 1979). Agricultural economics, although much more strongly developed, also has distinctive blind spots.

This does not mean that no work on labor in agriculture has been undertaken either in agricultural economics, rural sociology, or in related disciplines in the social sciences. In California, for example, Fuller[2] and others in agricultural economics have addressed the issue of agricultural labor. However, all too frequently, the analysis of this subject has fallen to scholars *outside* the confines of agricultural economics or rural sociology. Thus Paul Taylor[3] was one of the pioneers who worked on this subject but was located in a department of economics. Similarly, Clark Kerr collaborated with Taylor on one such study (Taylor and Kerr 1940) but also functioned outside a department of agricultural economics. Goldschmidt's studies conducted from *within* the agricultural sciences system, and his difficulties in publishing his findings, demonstrate the problems of conducting critical social research inside the system (Goldschmidt 1978; Friedland 1979).

More important, however, is the fact that many of the studies by agricultural economists of commodity production have been addressed almost exclusively to the question of labor *costs*, ignoring a host of other issues including the organization of the production process; the social organization of the workplace; the question of supply; and the interaction of workers, supervisors, and employers.

In our topic, lettuce, for example, a great deal is known about the comparative costs of packing in different ways (Smith et al. 1955; Enochian et al. 1955, 1957) or the risks and uncertainties in growing lettuce (Moore and Snyder 1969). Similarly, there exist overall studies of the lettuce production system (Wellman 1926; Jones and Tavernetti 1932) but there are no studies that address the factor of labor as a crucial element in production.[4]

The paucity of studies relating to labor is notable not only in lettuce as an agricultural commodity but in agriculture more generally. It is our contention that this is not accidental. Not only have rural sociologists and agricultural economists stayed away from this topic but the state of data collection concerning labor is primitive because this body of information has constituted a "dangerous" topical area. As will be shown in Chapter 3 when we discuss the question of the numbers of workers entailed, the lack of information is not unintentional. The present study will involve an area long defined as difficult and avoided by social scientists. This avoidance is a product of the existence of a powerfully organized constituency, growers and processors, who have provided indications to the social science "community" of their preferences – that labor not be studied by scientists in agriculture. In this respect, then, lettuce is not an unusual agricultural commodity: A cursory examination of research in rural sociology demonstrates that a host of controversial topics, especially those involving labor, have been carefully avoided for many decades (Friedland 1979).

Despite these obstacles, social projection requires that we turn to controversial areas and expose ourselves to a variety of criticisms. We believe that this process will facilitate the development of a projective methodology because there exist organized groups with differential interests in the commodity system, and that the expressions by these groups around the projections contained in this study will strengthen scientific efforts.

A methodology for social projection

In this study three approaches to the development of a projective methodology[5] will be used:

Projective analysis must be comparative, utilizing post-factum analyses of other comparable systems, setting out the differences and similarities.

Projective analysis must deal with totalities of a system; in agricultural commodities this will refer to production, processing, and distribution in most cases.

Projective analysis must be grounded in historical study. No production and distribution system exists except in an historical and systemic context. Any analysis that ignores such factors and concentrates on the here and now, and/or the immediate, can only make limited projections about the impact of technological change. The utilization of historical analysis will demonstrate the value of the development of a typology of change and will conclude this methodological examination with a consideration of two types of change: *incremental* and *transformational*.

Comparative analysis and projective methodology

The use of the comparative method is basic to many of the social sciences. Our intention here is not to review the variety of comparative methods that can be found but to make explicit the *particular* method of comparison we will utilize in formulating our social impact assessment.

First, our comparative analysis will involve the delineation of the totality of one system, lettuce, and the near totality of a second system, processing tomatoes. More accurately, we have sought to include as much of the totality that we have been able to comprehend with finite time and resources. The explicit comparisons between the two production systems will be made in the concluding chapter; here we are primarily concerned with specifying methodological considerations. We should immediately make clear one caveat: Processing tomatoes has never been examined as a total system because previous work (Friedland and Barton 1975, 1976; Scheuring and Thompson 1978) has been limited to the production elements of the system and does not deal with either the processing or the distributional aspects. Analysis of distribution as a segment of this system may not be essential for our present task, but the processing of tomatoes is an important part of the entire system, although the examination of this segment of the total system has not yet been accomplished.

By comparison, the examination of lettuce as a system will involve production, distribution, and, to the extent that is important, processing. The processing of lettuce in the form of shredding is still not very significant, but it represents a "growth sector" of the industry and, in addition, is one that is particularly appropriate and accommodative to mechanized harvesting.

Second, comparative analysis of one "case" (tomatoes) suggests ways of focusing the study of a second system (lettuce). Such suggestions must, of course, be treated with caution. This point has both power and danger.

When dealing with systems that have some common features, we find that factors relevant in one system may be equally relevant in another. But systems are rarely totally, or even closely, equivalent. Tomatoes and lettuce are both agricultural crops: They require land preparation, seeding, irrigation, cultivation, harvesting, handling, and so on. The experiences developed by a post-factum analysis in one can be useful; but depending on the similarities can also have its dangers. For example, tomatoes are a "once-over" crop: Once the field has been harvested there is no returning to that field for more tomatoes. Lettuce is, in contrast, a recurrent crop in which the vegetable is harvested in several passes through the field. Tomatoes are grown on a production schedule to produce a field for a distribution schedule, for example, a single date, whereas the production schedule of lettuce requires that it be harvested on a continuous basis for year-round delivery.

Comparative analysis directs us, therefore, to *analytic foci*, that is, the experience in one system instructs us to look for similarities in another. Perhaps the best example of this is demonstrated by the handling problem. In the case of tomatoes the handling of the fruit after harvest was not delineated as a problem until after the technology of fruit breeding and mechanical harvesting was completed. It was then discovered that the capacity of the machine to harvest fruit far surpassed the capacity to handle it. In the case of the lettuce harvester, handling consequently was recognized as a major problem and became part of the research design of the whole mechanized harvesting problem.

The concept of *analytic focus* can also serve other heuristic purposes: It suggests that questions be raised about segments of the system that will "fit together" most appropriately with those segments that appear ready for change. We will see, for example, in the examination of lettuce production, that one segment of the system that is being developed experimentally, seedlings production and transplantation, could fit together remarkably well with mechanized harvesting.

The crux of a projective methodology is the examination of, and extrapolation from, similarities and dissimilarities among a number of cases. In the examination of a particular case, certain characteristics, or analytic foci, can be identified. As more cases are added for examination, these analytic foci can be compared to determine their generic features. This implies that the original cases will be post-factum analyses from which movement occurs toward cases in which projection will be attempted. By examining the stages of development of the various analytic foci of post-factum cases and applying similar analyses to developing cases, one sees the prospect emerge for making projections based on the probabilities and rates of change. Such projections cannot be considered as either absolute or specific but rather as indicative. For example, if we consider the analytic focus of mechanization in several specific cases, the examination of various preconditions for a transition to mechanization makes it possible to assess preconditions in other cases.

The use of analytic foci developed through comparative analysis then sustains the next process in social projection: the exploration of various outcomes based on certain explicit assumptions. Here the process is one of utilizing conjectures, for example, if-then propositions, and scenarios. (Miller 1977; Vlachos 1977). The process involves:

1. Explicit delineation of "reasonable" assumptions.
2. Setting out of the range of alternatives based on each assumption.
3. Delineation of the potential consequences of each assumption.
4. Consideration of the chain(s) of consequences for each immediate consequence.

System, totality, and projective methodology

The notion of the need for totality in analysis is well established in the social sciences. Even before Lewin (1951) developed this idea in his gestalt psychology, the patterns of social analysis emphasizing the interrelationship of parts was well recognized, and the origins of the concept can be traced back to the very beginnings of social science. Similar applications of this methodology are also found in the sciences, for example, in the Heisenberg indeterminacy principle that stresses how examination of one phenomenon affects others (Heelan 1975). Indeed, even that relatively positivistic segment of sociology known as functionalism utilized gestalt principles in some of its key formative works. Thus when Malinowski (1948) studied the Trobrianders to discover the context of their use of magic and religion, he could make sense out of the parts only by considering the whole.

Although this point may be methodologically obvious, constant restatement is required because it is as frequently ignored as it is repeated. Thus one of the directives that flow from this methodology presses us to avoid focusing or concentrating on what might appear to be the most immediate, or dramatic, aspects of technological change. With a methodological obligation to delineate as completely as possible the parameters of a system, we have found ourselves being oriented to the conditions under which the harvest mechanization transition will occur. This will be, perhaps, best exemplified in the discussion in Chapter 4 of the potential effects of a rise in the cost of transportation.

In emphasizing the need for examination of the totality of a system, we must also acknowledge the difficulties in attempting to assess *all* factors involved in a given system. We recognize three distinctive limiting problems in grasping the whole or totality of a system in analyses such as we have conducted in lettuce.

1. In any given systemic analysis there can be too much and too little information. One problem is, therefore, information overload; its converse is the unavailability of data. We can illustrate this point by citing the enormous volume of literature dealing with diseases of lettuce and problems of decay after harvest. At the same time, practically nothing is known scientifically about lettuce harvest workers, their numbers, social characteristics, and so on. There is often a tendency, therefore, to focus on what is available rather than on what is, or could be, important.

2. Any analysis must come to grips with a variety of built-in blinders that potentially can exist. Some factors in any systemic analysis are taken so much for granted that their very significance is lost. For example, the handling of water is so routinized, and the infrastructure for its delivery so normalized, that it is easy to forget the potentialities of effects if blockages in its delivery were to occur. Similarly, lettuce as a production system obviously requires sizable volumes of capital; money must be borrowed from time to time by lettuce firms and repaid. What a sharp increase or decrease in the cost of obtaining capital might produce with respect to the totality of a system is difficult to determine. Moreover, information about this aspect of the system is not generally available. Like labor, information on the availabilies of capital and its usages is difficult to come by.

   We might also note the way in which disciplinary training can also develop sets of blinders. A discipline is, at one and the same time, a powerful directive to analysis but a set of limitations. Although as sociologists, we like to think of ourselves as being sensitive to economic factors, we have every reason to believe that a trained economist would have noted elements of lettuce as a system that we have ignored. The same would hold for agricultural engineers or geneticists.

3. A special set of constraints exists by virtue of the degree to which a given system in "open" or "closed." Some commodities, for example, are relatively open and considerable information is available about them.

The analysis of totalities, although seemingly obvious, is intended to alert readers to the needs and problems of such analysis. On the one hand, it is necessary to delineate the parameters of the system under consideration as broadly and in as much detail as possible. At the same time, researchers must be alert to the factors that can be overlooked, taken for granted, underrated, or inaccessible because of disciplinary bias or internal secrecy.

Historical analysis and projective methodology

The present study and the earlier *Destalking the Wily Tomato* (Friedland and Barton 1975) emphasize historical analysis by dedicating a section of each to the historical evolution of the commodity systems. This emphasis is, to a considerable degree, a product of the distinctive disciplinary outlook of much of sociology although, of course, historical perspectives are hardly a unique feature of this discipline.

The detailed consideration of the commodity system over time, however, has served not only to provide a contextual understanding for the perspective and the projections developed in this study but, in addition, shows how conceptualization of the change process can be facilitated. In this section we will demonstrate the heuristic character of historical analysis by developing a typology of change; this typology will make a distinction between *incremental* and *transformational* change. At the same time, the historical analysis will be shown to have been useful in the examination of the conditions for the transition to mechanized harvesting. It was this factor that led us to stress the need to examine the conditions of technological transitions, recognizing that historically such transitions do not simply occur because of the technological state of the art.

Most change that occurs in agriculture is *incremental*. The agricultural research and development system, as embodied particularly in the land grant colleges of agriculture, the State Agricultural Experiment Stations, and Extension, is an extensive network involved in a staggering variety of research and application endeavors. The bulk of research tends to produce a large number of small changes, each with small effects. Perhaps one example that might be cited is the ongoing research concerned with varieties. In processing tomatoes, for example, the original breeding research that gave rise to the V-145 variety has proliferated into a staggering number of descendants, each with its own special characteristics, utilities, benefits, and problems. In most cases, in tomatoes and other commodities, research into varieties produces seeds that fit the requirements of a given production system with marginal increments of improvement. Over time, such incremental improvement increases productivity. These increases are rarely dramatic, but occasionally they are. Most research is incremental, dealing with small but significant problems such as insects and/or fungi, increased output, improvement of quality and/or appearance of the commodity, and so on.

On some occasions, however, sometimes through deliberate search but often inadvertently, changes are introduced that are *transformational,* having ramifications throughout many segments of a production, processing, and distribution system. Historical analysis of two commodities, lettuce and tomatoes, will illustrate the interaction between incremental and transformational innovation and change. Historical analysis emphasizes two points that should be made explicit:

1. The typology we have developed of incremental-transformational changes must be thought of as ranging along a continuum rather than as a polarity. Although we recognize the rough character of the distinction between these types of technological change, we will use incremental and transformational change as a dichotomy for the dependent variable in the model presented in Chapter 1 (see Figure 1.1). Incremental change will represent a low value or ranking on the dependent variable; transformational change will represent a high value or ranking.
2. The development of the typology alerts the researcher to the limits of technology. It points out the need for the analysis of the conditions under which existing technology will be adopted and utilized and therefore possibly will create a new transformation of a system.

The work of social projection, if it is to become a standard aspect of scientific procedures, is not a simple one. In this study we will attempt to specify not only the methods for conducting such projective analyses but will also use a post-factum study to elucidate projection in another case.

This task is demanding because it requires that we go on record with respect to a controversial subject in which there are a considerable number of contentious and conflicting elements, groups, and organizations. It would be simpler, of course, to withdraw to the comparative safety of post-factum studies or genuinely "blue sky" predictions that are so global that they are beyond the possibility of empirical analysis in a reasonably short time frame. But, although this is one of the disadvantages of a projective orientation, we believe it necessary to undertake because without such experimentation – and we consider our work as social experimentation, not under laboratory but under *real* conditions – the social scientific enterprise is limited in its utility. Social science can and should be utilizable; it should facilitate the process by which different social forces can see the outcomes of action so that better public debate *and* controversy can occur. It is only through such analysis and debate that democratic processes can grow and become more meaningful. As long as processes are secretive, hidden, and inaccessible, social outcomes are produced in which the bulk of the affected people feel their control over their world is limited, negligible, or nonexistent. Through this study we hope to facilitate a process by which greater democratic participation can occur in our society.

Processing tomatoes: a case study for comparative analysis

Before turning to the detailed consideration of the social organization of lettuce production, we will discuss the social organization of tomato production and the social consequences of the shift to mechanized harvesting.[6]

Tomato production became a substantial and growing agricultural production sector in California following World War II. A labor-intensive crop requiring large numbers of workers for hand picking tomatoes increased in acreage in California until, by 1962, over 177,000 acres were harvested. These enormous acreages involved approximately 4,000 growers and required about 50,000 workers in the harvest. Many plots were fairly small and growers could plant varying acreages of tomatoes, coordinating them with other crops.

Until 1964 the supply of labor was unlimited, in effect, because growers could resolve their labor requirements by ordering braceros through the intergovernmental arrangements then in effect. The bracero program, however, came under increasing criticism in the 1950s, and by the early 1960s it was becoming clear that a major transition in the labor supply was about to occur.

In preparation for this transition, a search had begun for a mechanized harvesting system for tomatoes involving a new tomato variety capable of being machine harvested and a machine capable of harvesting tomatoes.

The new system, developed at the University of California, Davis, was ready for adoption by 1961 but was not acceptable to growers while the bracero program continued. By 1965, when the growers were cut off from the Mexican labor supply, a rapid transition to the machine occurred.

This transition had substantial ramifications throughout the entire tomato production system. Table 4.2 shows that a complete transition took place between 1964 when only 3.8 percent of the crop was machine harvested and 1969 when less than 1 percent continued to be hand harvested. The rapidity of the transition constitutes an interesting chapter in research and development in agricultural technology.

Research for this transition began when a plant breeder at Davis began a search for a potential tomato variety that could be machine harvested before World War II. After the war an agricultural engineer was drawn into the research and a ten-year project got under way, which resulted in a machine-harvestable tomato plant and a machine prototype.

The consequences of the transition to mechanized harvesting were significant. These included: the concentration of tomato growing in California; the concentration of production among a small number of growers; a shift in the location of tomato production; the inception of price bargaining, although only weakly, between growers and processors; significant changes in the numbers of workers and in the composition of the labor force; and the retention of primitive industrial relations accompanying technological sophistication.

Concentration of tomato growing in California

Although California's share of national production of processing tomatoes increased steadily from 1949 (39.8 percent of U.S. production) to 1964 (65.8 percent), California growers feared that the end of the bracero program would result in a move by tomato processors to Mexico, because it was believed that California's growing significance in tomato production was based on the regular, predictable, and cheap labor supply of Mexican braceros. Without these workers there was general belief in the industry that the processors would move facilities to Mexico and encourage the development of production below the border.

The speedy adoption of an existing technology and its rapid refinement through continuous and intensive research and development made California even more effective in tomato production. By 1974 California tonnage constituted 83.3 percent of national production and its share of the market has remained in this area.

At the same time, U.S. production, in terms of acreage and tonnage, increased between 1964 and 1974 by 175 and 201 percent, respectively. Thus the machine harvesting system introduced significant changes in the structure of tomato production nationally.

Concentration of tomato growers

Although tomato production concentrated in California, it also produced important changes in the process of growing, which was manifested dramatically in the decline in numbers of tomato producers. In 1962 there were approximately 4,000 growers of processing tomatoes in California. By 1973 their number had declined to 597 although, as previously noted, acreage and tonnage had increased significantly.

These changes were a product of the increased capital costs to remain in tomato production, as well as the higher levels of technological sophistication required of growers remaining in tomato production. With the initial cost of a harvesting machine at $25,000 and rising rapidly, it made little sense to continue tomato production unless acreages would be concomitant with the capacity of the machine. Thus the smaller farms of some growers ceased to be economically viable. As the capacity of the machine (and the price) increased, growers had to increase the number of acres planted to tomatoes.

In addition, tomato production became increasingly specialized as growers had to commit themselves to delivery of the fruit on a scheduled basis in their contracts with processors. Considerable research and development at the University of California, Davis, and by extension agents in counties heavily committed to tomato production was undertaken to meet this problem and quickly led to greater predictability and control. The new technology involved much closer care and attention to every phase of production and some growers were unable to make the transition to factorylike production processes.

Creating the basis for price bargaining

Prior to 1974 the California Tomato Growers Association (CTGA), the only crop-based organization of full- and part-time tomato growers, had been unsuccessful in its attempts to organize growers for collective price bargaining with processors. Tomato growers, through the association and labor supply organizations, had been able to regulate wage rates under the bracero program but faced regulation themselves when it came to the oligopoly of tomato processors and canners. Processors wielded power over the growers by virtue of their control over access to processing, that is, by reason of the enormous capital investment necessary to start a cannery or processing unit, even a cooperative one. The processors also maintained a firmly entrenched market position, controlling distribution, marketing, and advertising networks. Although it is not possible to produce legal evidence of collusive behavior among the processors, it is clear that producers were whipsawed by the processors over the contracted prices for tomatoes; that is, contracts for future production were allocated by the processors prior to the beginning of each season.

With the decreased number and the increased size of individual producing firms, however, growers found it possible to develop sufficient group interest to bargain with some degree of effectiveness. Although the canneries continue to mediate demand for tomatoes, the CTGA has experienced greater success in bargaining over contract prices for its members.

Shift in locations of production

Accompanying the other shifts among growers was the shift in geographical locations of production within California. Originally, tomato production was centered close to the delta area in California, where the Sacramento and San Joaquin rivers enter San Francisco Bay. Although some of the farms producing tomatoes held, through direct ownership or lease, considerable acreages in this area, the majority of production was located in a hodgepodge of relatively small owner-farmed plots. The new scale of production facilitated by machine harvesting stimulated a minor land rush in the state.

The preconditions for a geographical shift were augmented by the development of irrigation and transportation facilities on the west side of the San Joaquin Valley, an area previously devoted to cattle grazing and other forms of dry farming because of its aridity and isolation, During the late 1950s and early 1960s the massive California Water Project brought federal and state subsidized water to the area from northern California. At the same time, a new highway, Interstate 5, was being built to replace the insignificant secondary road serving the west side of the valley. With water, transportation, and a machine that required reduced numbers of harvest workers, Fresno County rapidly became a major producer of tomatoes.

The changing character of the labor force

Whereas some 50,000 workers (overwhelmingly, if not entirely, composed of male Mexican braceros) had hand harvested the tomatoes until 1964, the end of the bracero program and the shift to mechanized harvesting changed the numbers and composition of the harvest labor force drastically.

Decreasing to an estimated 18,000 by 1972, the number of harvesters dropped again after 1975 when electronic sorting was introduced. In the first change, growers recruited a predominantly local labor force composed overwhelmingly of women. Many were housewives entering tomato harvesting to augment family incomes. With electronic harvesting, machines with increased harvesting capacity required only five or six workers, compared to the sixteen to twenty-four hand sorters required, a drop to between one-quarter to one-third of what was previously needed.

Technological sophistication and primitive labor relations

Although growers found themselves with a highly complex technological production system, many were unable to grasp the complexities of dealing with their labor force. Accustomed to the unlimited supply and control over labor of the bracero program, and reflecting the continuance of a seemingly unlimited labor supply through illegal immigration, growers generally assumed the labor supply was assured and that little adaptation would be required to deal with the workers required to staff the mechanical harvesters.

It was not until the United Farm Workers essayed an attempt at organizing tomato workers in 1975 that growers began to treat the labor market as problematic. Their response, on the whole, however, was not to seek means to develop a regularized supply of dependable labor but to adopt a new technology replacing still more workers. This was accomplished by fitting electronic sorters to the machines (Scheuring and Thompson 1978). The sorter is a device that sorts tomatoes according to the color of the fruit, rejecting green fruit and/or objects not showing an appropriate degree of redness.

In some cases of large growers involved in a diversified growing program, the requisite numbers of workers for the new electronic system were drawn from permanent workers and their families. Other growers continued to depend on a seasonal labor force but the numbers of workers required were much reduced. Thus adoption of this second generation of technological innovation correlated with a belief on the part of the growers that machines were preferable to dealings with organized workers, a belief that is not unique to agricultural employers.

The tomato case study demonstrates how major transformations of the production process occur when the labor supply or control over labor become uncertain. At the same time, the case shows the specific changes that are effected in all aspects of the production system.

The tomato case study demonstrates how the replacement of labor by capital-intensive technology produces significant ramifications in a production system. The consequences of mechanized harvesting included not only the displacement of the braceros but also the processes of concentration that reshaped the entire production system. As will be seen in Chapter 3, similar transformational changes have developed in the production of lettuce in the past. Mechanized harvesting of lettuce, a technological development that already exists, has not yet been adopted and transformed the lettuce production system. In the next two chapters we will examine the system of producing lettuce as a market commodity, the conditions under which harvest mechanization will occur, and the consequences that we expect will result from mechanization.

3. The social organization of lettuce production

Lettuce as a commodity system

Lettuce production and distribution constitutes a single complex system developed over the past five decades. Its complexity derives largely from the fact that over 85 percent of U.S. lettuce, an extremely delicate agricultral commodity with a very short storability capacity, is produced in California and Arizona and distributed nationally, over distances of thousands of miles, to hundreds of markets in the United States.

A general process of internationalization of fresh commodity production is also occurring in lettuce. Not only is U.S. lettuce shipped to Canada but increasing volumes are being sold to markets in Asia (especially Hong Kong and Japan) and Europe, although exports still constitute only a small fragment of U.S. total production. One U.S. firm regularly airfreights lettuce to Germany for McDonald's hamburgers.

Unlike stable agricultural commodities such as wheat, corn, and soybeans, which can be stored for long periods, lettuce is unusually perishable. If chilled immediately after harvest and maintained at carefully controlled temperatures above freezing, lettuce can last three weeks. This life span is jeopardized by even slight rises in temperatures. The complexity of the lettuce production and distribution system, then, is an inevitable feature of the characteristics of the commodity. In this respect lettuce is similar to most fresh market vegetables and fruits but is notably more delicate than all except a few others, for example, strawberries.

Problems of delicacy are tied to those of growth rates. Lettuce grows at different rates depending on variety, temperature, weather conditions, and other factors including cultivation and irrigation, and thus no field of lettuce ever matures homogeneously. A field will approach maturity but on any given day only a certain percentage of the heads will be ready for harvest. The state of the market and the supply of labor available, therefore, become important factors in the decision to begin harvesting. Because of these many factors, lettuce production is a highly complex process: Each individual grower plans to bring a given area of lettuce to harvest at a definite target period. Planning will take into consideration the estimated time required to grow the lettuce, guesses about the state of the market and what other growers will be doing around that period, and many other factors.

The complexity of planning creates a distinctiveness about lettuce that is remarkable when compared to other fresh market commodity production systems. For one thing, lettuce production is dominated by a relatively small number of firms generically referred to as *grower-shippers*. These firms both grow and ship lettuce; they also contract with individual farmers to grow lettuce for them to pack and ship.

As is typical with much of American agriculture, the growing of lettuce is a specialized process in which most lettuce grower-shippers concentrate on the growing of lettuce and a number of additional crops, almost invariably fresh vegetables, such as asparagus, broccoli, cauliflower, celery, or spinach. Not all grower-shippers will grow all these crops; but most will produce some crops other than lettuce and market them through their firms. The growth of other crops serves a variety of purposes for growers and grower-shippers: It may be useful in terms of rotating crops, scheduling crops according to growth cycles so that more than a single crop can be grown in a season, fitting labor requirements together to obtain maximum utilization of permanent employees, as well as shipping mixed loads of different crops.

For most grower-shippers, however, lettuce is the prime crop and its production has a distinctive image within the agricultural community. Lettuce grower-shippers have a reputation for being risk-taking entrepreneurs notable in an economic sector that prides itself for living with the ambiguities of weather and the uncertainties of the market. Among themselves and in agriculture generally, lettuce growers are often regarded as "gamblers."

This designation is, at one and the same time, accurate and illusory. Lettuce is a more speculative commodity than most other agricultural products. When producing a crop, the lettuce grower does not know whether the crop will be an economic disaster at $2.50 a carton or will be "green gold" at $15.00. To operate under these circumstances, lettuce-producing firms must develop internal organizational and capital capacities to function continuously for long periods with great uncertainty and unusual variation in market conditions.

If lettuce production is a gambler's occupation, it is now rare that individual gamblers can "take a flyer" in lettuce. Most lettuce is produced through highly specialized firms – the grower-shippers – that grow and market lettuce, although occasional individuals may seek entry into its production. The designation of lettuce growers as "gamblers" is thus partially accurate but it should be remembered that the gamblers are rarely individuals, but sizable firms.

Beyond the special characteristics of lettuce as a gambler's crop, lettuce production requires integration and scheduling that is remarkable in agricultural production. As a result of decades of scientific research, much of which was publicly funded through the U.S. Department of Agriculture and the state Agriculture Experiment Stations, growers have learned how to control many of the factors involved in lettuce production.[1] Despite this, uncertainties remain fundamental to lettuce growing: A few days' rise or fall in temperature can produce sizable volumes of lettuce, thereby dropping prices precipitously, or considerable shortages with skyrocketing prices. If volume is heavy but labor is in short supply and/or equipment, cooling, or transportation is unavailable, the capacity of the grower-shipper to harvest and market is severely affected.

Lettuce production must be planned and scheduled despite the uncertainties, therefore, very much like production in any complex assembly operation. There are differences, of course: Workers are brought to the product rather than vice versa (as in most manufacturing operations); the volume of parts that require integration is much smaller than in most manufacturing operations; and the perishability of products in manufacturing is much lower than that found in lettuce production. Despite these differences, the capital requirements necessary for equipment and the ability to survive through long periods in which the "green gold" has turned to dross through low markets have created a situation in which a relatively small number of firms grow and handle the overwhelming bulk of American lettuce. It is these complex factors that have given rise to the distinctive form of production, grower-shipper firms, and the integrated transportation network, extending from point of production to point of sale, from "seed to supermarket."[2]

The structure of the lettuce system

The size of the lettuce production system is suggested by the fact that in 1976 119,076 carlots of lettuce were harvested and marketed in the United States. A carlot is equivalent in most states to 1,000 cartons. One way to develop perspective is to compare lettuce with other commodities and firms. Because almost all grower-shippers are private firms or subsidiaries of larger corporate entities that do not report on their subsidiaries specifically, only some rough comparisons can be made. The total dollar volume of production for all firms in 1977 was $473,837,000. It must be remembered, however, that we are discussing a single fresh vegetable, even though one in widespread use. Although lettuce-producing firms are not so important as the top-rankers in *Fortune* magazine's top five hundred corporations, they are significantly large organizations within agriculture.

One important aspect of the structure of lettuce production is its degree of geographical concentration. Tables 3.1 and 3.2 provide data on this concentration. Table 3.1 shows California and Arizona production of lettuce and the percentage the two states constitute of U.S. production. Table 3.2 shows the dollar value of lettuce by major California production districts as well as for California, Arizona, and the United States.[3] Tables 3.1 and 3.2 show that California and Arizona produced 89 percent of U.S. volume and 80 percent of the dollar value in 1976.

The data not only reveal the significance of California and Arizona but demonstrate another important fact about lettuce production: It is an integrated, year-round system linked to a large number of urban markets throughout the United States.

Because lettuce is provided in all these markets on a *daily* basis, production has been concentrated, a process facilitated by the development in the 1920s of a national distribution system, originally based on railways and, since the 1950s, geared to trucks and trailers. This system is also used to distribute other fresh vegetables and some fruits, some of which are produced by lettuce grower-shippers.

A second structural feature of lettuce production is its high degree of concentration. Table 3.3 shows the number of firms in lettuce production and their shares of the California market.[4] This table shows that twelve handlers were responsible for 51 percent of California iceberg volume and that twenty-nine handlers produced 77 percent of California production.

Our own knowledge of the field indicates that four of the largest handlers are, in fact, grower-shippers who probably are responsible for shipping about 40 percent of California–Arizona lettuce. The degree of concentration in lettuce, although perhaps not so significant as the degree of concentration in industries such as steel, autos, tractors, and the like, is, nevertheless, remarkable for the production of fresh foods.

Table 3.1. *California, Arizona, and U.S. Production of Lettuce by Volume, Annually*

	1969	1970	1971	1972	1973	1974	1975	1976
California	63,217	68,481	68,093	77,461	77,678	79,931	85,915	86,961
Arizona	22,135	19,463	20,682	19,194	18,696	18,422	17,586	18,177
California & Arizona	85,352	87,944	88,775	96,655	96,374	98,353	103,501	105,138
Other U.S.	12,877	11,717	11,506	11,441	12,880	10,818	12,344	13,938
Total U.S.	98,229	99,661	100,281	108,096	109,254	109,171	115,845	119,076
California % of U.S.	64.4	68.7	67.9	71.7	71.1	73.2	74.2	73.0
Arizona % of U.S.	22.5	19.5	20.6	17.8	17.1	16.9	15.2	15.3
Calif/Ariz % of U.S.	86.9	88.2	88.5	89.4	88.2	90.1	89.3	88.3
Other U.S. % of U.S.	13.1	11.8	11.5	10.6	11.8	9.9	10.7	11.7

Numbers represent "standard carlots" = 1,000 cartons of lettuce

Source: Federal-State Market News Service, *Marketing Lettuce from Salinas-Watsonville-King City and Other Central California Districts,* annual reports, 1969–77.

Table 3.2. *Lettuce Dollar Value (× 000), Major California Production Districts, California, Arizona, and U.S., by Year*

District and county	1969	1970	1971	1972	1973	1974	1975	1976
Salinas Valley								
Monterey	49,040	62,620	65,800	64,222	118,765	114,894	100,620	155,712
Santa Cruz	4,149	5,128	5,565	6,420	10,267	8,783	8,395	13,118
San Benito	1,716	3,370	2,820	3,320	4,290	4,380	3,560	5,038
Desert								
Imperial	38,683	31,373	44,795	60,136	73,200	50,476	75,180	69,365
Riverside	12,562	8,197	4,656	6,625	12,267	3,895	11,476	16,522
Santa Maria								
San Luis Obispo	5,075	7,034	8,185	8,179	14,155	11,104	12,644	17,488
Santa Barbara	3,855	6,371	7,969	8,660	19,830	13,580	12,302	17,953
Total Arizona	68,106	40,282	60,038	58,607	58,059	54,932	61,424	52,232
Total California	134,970	148,104	180,234	183,287	260,727	247,976	250,343	324,778
Total U.S.	241,059	223,276	281,719	278,736	374,923	355,536	365,608	473,837
California % of U.S.	56.0	66.3	64.0	65.8	69.5	69.7	68.5	68.5
Calif/Ariz % of U.S.	84.2	84.4	85.3	86.8	85.0	85.2	85.3	79.6

Sources: County data from County Agricultural Commissioners. Arizona, California, and U.S. data from Federal-State Market News Service, *Marketing Lettuce from Salinas-Watsonville-King City and Other Central California Districts*, annual reports, 1969–76.

Table 3.3. *Number of Lettuce Handling Firms and Share of Market by Firm Size*

| Number of carlot[a] handled | Handlers | | Carlots volume | Percent of total volume | Cumulative percentage |
	Number	Percent of total			
3,000 or more	3	4	23,544.6	27	27
2,000–2,999	9	10	20,897.2	24	51
1,000–1,999	17	20	22,192.8	26	77
500–999	18	21	11,434.5	13	90
5–499	39	45	8,809.2	10	100

[a]1 carlot = 1,000 cartons
Source: California Iceberg Lettuce Research Program, cited in Drossler 1976, p. 18.

The production and distribution system

It would be useful, in dealing with the totality of lettuce as a system to divide it into two subsystems, production and distribution.

Production

The production system constitutes the entire process by which capital is translated through land and other factors of production into a finished product, lettuce packed in cartons, chilled, and ready for shipment. The assemblage of the various factors of production depends almost entirely on firms referred to as grower-shippers who bring together capital, land, equipment, labor, materials, transportation, and additional factors in such a way that lettuce can be shipped on a continual basis throughout the year.

Land is assembled in a variety of ways. In 1962, for example, about half the lettuce grown in the Salinas Valley was grown by small growers whereas the other half was grown by grower-shippers (Moore and Snyder 1969, p. 3). Some grower-shippers own land and lease additional acreage whereas others own little or none and lease their entire acreage. Three basic arrangements can be found, involving (1) ownership, (2) leasing, and (3) some form of joint venture. Joint ventures involve contracts between grower and grower-shipper with respect to marketing.

In marketing, Moore and Synder (1969) noted five types of marketing arrangements in the Salinas Valley:

1. Marketing through a cooperative. All the operating capital is furnished by the grower and none of the proceeds are shared.
2. A joint venture with a shipper. The shipper advances one-half the cultural costs to purchase a 50-percent share in the crop. Returns are split equally from the first carton harvested. The balance of the operating capital must be furnished by the grower from his or her own sources.
3. Lettuce is grown under a contract with a packer. A $135 per acre advance is made to the grower and the packer furnishes one-half the cost of pesticides and fertilizer. Returns are split after the cost of the shipper's share of pesticides and fertilizer are returned.
4. A minimum income guarantee contract with the packer. All the hoeing and thinning costs and $135 are advanced. Receipts are shared equally after the $135 is returned.
5. A flat fee of $300 per acre is paid to the grower to produce an acre of lettuce. There is no sharing of profits or losses by the grower.

The complexities of arrangements in the Salinas Valley are probably found also in other lettuce-producing districts. However, it should be noted that different conditions exist in other places, which affect the way arrangements are made. One grower-shipper, for example, may lease land exclusively in the Salinas Valley but own acreage in the Imperial Valley. One medium-sized grower, in contrast, owns acreage in Salinas but must work out leasing and joint ventures to produce lettuce during the winter-production season.

In preparation for lettuce production and during its planting and cultivation, sizable amounts of equipment are required. Land must be planed to permit irrigation. Land planing involves the use of heavy tractor-drawn equipment. Of course, any land used for lettuce must be linked to a complex infrastructure that delivers water to the specific plot where lettuce is produced. When the land surface is ready, planting beds must be formed utilizing other heavy equipment. When the beds are shaped, the seed can be planted, again involving specialized equipment that not only plants the seeds but often applies fertilizers, herbicides, and pesticides simultaneously. During growth, water must be applied periodically.

Table 3.4. *Harvest Equipment Used by Three Arizona Lettuce Firms, 1963*

	Company G	Company H	Company I
Wrap machines	9		
Stitcher trucks	5	4	2
Wide wheel trucks	17	7	5
Pickup trucks	12	6	2
Crew buses	8	3	4
Portable parts houses	3		
Humps (wheelbarrows)	200	100	75
Clamps (box closers)	200	35	25
Spray cans	150		
Staple guns	150	40	15
Cutting knives	500	262	100
Flat bed trucks (1 ton)		1	
Wide-track trailers		3	
Gas engines		10	
Water cans			12
Hatchets			9
Files			72
Stitching machines			4
Lettuce acreage worked	1,120	5,597	1,688
Cartons shipped	1,587,019	3,277,904	423,182

Source: Padfield and Martin 1965, pp. 51–73

The heaviest use of equipment occurs with the harvest. In addition to a variety of trucks and tractors, specialized wrapping machines are often utilized as well as a variety of heavy and light tools. Table 3.4 shows the equipment used in Arizona by three companies studied in 1963 by Padfield and Martin (1965).

Another way to gain some idea of the volume of equipment necessary for harvest is to utilize the information made available by one firm in an insert advertisement to *The Packer*, December 24, 1974, the trade newspaper of the fresh fruit and vegetable industry. Mel Finerman, then one of the larger lettuce grower-shippers, shipped 9.25 million cartons of lettuce in 1974. "To accomplish that job it took an average weekly employment of from 650 to 950 workers with 2000 employed during peak weeks and 5,200 different individuals earning enough during the year to require as many W-2 earnings statements."

In 1974 Finerman operated ten wrapping machines, specially designed machines built on trucks. These trucks carry folding booms that are lowered to form conveyors straddling many rows of lettuce. Workers walk the rows, cutting the lettuce and lifting it on to the conveyors mounted on the booms. The lettuce then moves to the truck body where it is wrapped and packed into cartons. Finerman's machines were designed by company personnel in conjunction with a Chicago engineering firm and cost $65,000 each but would cost "$10,000 to 20,000 more to build now due to inflation."

To cool the lettuce after harvesting and packing, the firm owned its own vacuum coolers. "The equipment consists of three half-car vacuum tubes and four quarter-car tubes. All of the equipment is portable and can be moved from district to district . . ." The firm also owned a cool room at Yuma, Arizona, and expected to build additional cooling sites in all its major production districts.

To haul the lettuce from the fields, Finerman owned twenty-one specially designed trucks. A number of forklift trucks were also maintained to haul palletized lettuce cartons from trucks to coolers and then to trailers or railroad cars. In addition to this heavy equipment, Finerman noted the need for smaller equipment and tools, including wheelbarrows, templates for closing cartons, staplers, and so on.

Packing lettuce also involves a considerable volume of materials. The Finerman advertisement noted that:

cartons [are] delivered to the carton yard in units of 500,000 at a time. A daily inventory is kept and an actual physical inventory is taken every week. Staples are delivered in units of 35 million at a time. Wire for the stiching (sic!) machines is delivered in 20,000-lb. units . . . Each truck has on its bed 10 48 by 48 pallets. The packages are loaded on the pallets 32 to each pallet making a total load of 320 cartons.

Other materials are also necessary for wrapping the lettuce.

Distribution

The sale and distribution of lettuce involves a complex network of sellers and buyers as well as a national system for its handling and distribution. The sales and distribution system must articulate immediately with the production system because lettuce has only short storage capacity. Indeed, lettuce must be moved, almost as soon as it is harvested, through the process of cooling and then into transportation. Because lettuce matures on a schedule over which growers have only minimal control and must be harvested quickly after it matures, it can be available in large or small quantities at any given moment. Dependent on production and demand, sales personnel maintain immediate contact with production capacity; this tends to influence the state of the market almost immediately. Lettuce is a highly volatile crop in terms of price, which can shift within hours; it is not unknown for lettuce to double or halve its price within a period of several days.

The sale of lettuce is of sufficient importance so that most grower-shippers maintain their own sales organizations. Medium-sized grower-shippers more normally sell their lettuce through sales agents, for example, firms that specialize in the sale of lettuce and other fresh vegetables on behalf of a number of growers or grower-shippers. A number of other types of organizations that essentially function as sales agents also exist, but legal controls require the use of a variety of designations.

The buyers of lettuce (and other fresh vegetables) are somewhat more complex than the sellers; there are, after all, a relatively small number of lettuce sellers nationally. Lettuce buyers, however, exist in great numbers throughout the country. Of considerable importance is the fact that although lettuce sellers may specialize in lettuce (besides selling other crops), lettuce buyers rarely are specialized; most are buyers of a great variety of fresh commodities – vegetables and fruits – of which lettuce constitutes only one part. Basically, however, there are three types of lettuce buyers.

Supermarkets constitute one major buyer. Because supermarkets often purchase lettuce for a network of retail stores, they often buy the vegetable in sizable quantities. Some supermarket chains are so large that they maintain their own buying agents to deal with purchases of lettuce and other vegetables and fruits. Many supermarket chains are smaller, however, and will buy directly from grower-shippers.

Smaller supermarket chains that are localized to an area or smaller markets often buy their lettuce through firms in terminal markets, the second major grouping of lettuce buyers. Terminal markets are physical locations at which fresh produce is handled. Also, at such terminals there are a profusion of agents that buy and resell produce; these include brokers, agents, wholesalers, and others. Terminal market agents such as brokers will often assess the needs for lettuce and serve as buyers in bulk of one or more carlots of lettuce, which are then broken down into smaller parcels for delivery to wholesalers and/or retailers.

The third lettuce purchaser type is the institutional user. Some institutions, such as the Department of Defense, are so large that they purchase directly from grower-shippers. Other institutions purchase through terminal agents. Some institutional users have shifted from the purchase of ordinary lettuce to shredded lettuce – lettuce that has been processed either locally or at the source by removing the core and then running it through equipment that shreds it. Shredded lettuce is now being manufactured by some grower-shippers but more often is produced by local firms for local institutions.

The handling of lettuce after harvest involves its movement from the fields and its immediate chilling through a process of vacuum cooling. After chilling, lettuce is moved immediately to cold storage or, preferably, direct to the vehicles necessary for its movement. Transportation occurs in two basic forms: rail and truck, although a combination of the two also occurs through the use of piggyback trailers hauled for long distances before being used as trailers for short distance haul.

Rail transport was originally the most important form of transportation. Since the 1950s, however, with the development of the Interstate Highway System, truck transportation has grown in significance. Table 3.5 shows the relative importance of the two forms of transportation and the growth of truck transport for California lettuce.

A complex of transportation brokers and personnel are involved in the transportation of lettuce. The scheduling of railway cars ("reefers") and trailers is complicated and is often handled by specialist agencies. One firm maintains a fleet of its own trailers and, indeed, does a fair amount of rail piggyback transportation to the Midwest, beyond which it hauls its produce by truck. In addition to brokers, there are hauling firms, truckers, and others involved in lettuce transportation. Railway transport is also complex and entails considerable planning because lettuce must be delivered on a predictable schedule to markets at distances involving thousands of miles. Whether moved by rail, trailer, or combination, temperature control must be continually maintained throughout the movement phase. Not only must temperature be controlled but it must be controlled within a few degrees; there is little leeway available because a few degrees rise in temperature will drastically shorten the shelf life of the lettuce, whereas a few degrees of temperature drop will freeze it and turn it into slime. Temperature control must be maintained whether lettuce is moved through intense cold in the winter or the high temperatures of summer.

Once lettuce is delivered to a terminal, either a produce terminal of a

Table 3.5. *California Lettuce Transportation, Truck and Rail, Annual*

	1969	1970	1971	1972	1973	1974	1975	1976
Rail	32,733	34,329	29,405	32,357	27,017	27,097	23,873	15,606
Truck	30,485	34,322	38,750	44,775	50,675	52,836	61,981	71,355
Percent truck transport	48.2	50.0	56.9	58.0	65.2	66.1	72.2	82.1

Numbers of carlots at 1,000 cartons = carlot
Source: Federal-State Market News Service, *Marketing Lettuce from Salinas-Watsonville-King City and Other Central California Districts,* annual report, 1969–76.

supermarket chain or a large institutional user, or to a terminal market, it must be moved from the temperature control of the transport medium to cold storage with equivalent temperature control. Lettuce is then moved by local vehicles and trailers to retail stores or the cold rooms of institutional users. Again, temperature control is crucial. If lettuce is left standing around in summer heat, it quickly loses its coolness and the process of decay begins. Thus a considerable amount of energy must be devoted to scheduling the movement of lettuce in cold storage units.

Labor as a factor of production

Not only is the assemblage of land, equipment, and materials complicated, but the organization of the labor force is also complex. As is the case with agricultural production, but in contrast to most other production systems, labor inputs are not a constant element. Labor is required intensively at some periods in the production cycle but, at other times, is hardly required at all. This special character of labor requirements has been handled traditionally in agriculture, and in lettuce production, largely through the maintenance of a supply of *surplus* labor that can be available when necessary and which is *external* to the production firms. Only a very small segment of the labor force needed by any firm is composed of permanent employees, *internal* and integrated in the firm as regular employees. At this writing (1980), labor is organized in three distinct ways.

The internalized labor force

Internal workers are employees engaged in management, sales, supervision, and maintenance activities. In addition, however, there are other permanent employees such as tractor drivers, cooler operators, forklift operators, loaders, and others. Most of the workers, who move with the production season to appropriate sites to perform their work, are employed on a year-round basis. Others may not move seasonally but have vested and permanent job rights. Each growing-shipping firm maintains a sizable internalized labor force, which is rarely seen in the fields. An office staff is required, for example, for control, supervision, and planning, as well as for the maintenance of financial records. A sales staff rarely leaves the central office but is maintained on a continuous basis because lettuce is sold almost every day of every week of the year.

The externalized labor force

This consists of workers involved at various times in the production cycle, particularly with respect to thinning and weeding activities. In the planting and cultivation of lettuce, despite considerable research and development of both precision planting techniques and the application of herbicides, most lettuce must be thinned and weeded once during the growth cycle. This is a labor-intensive operation, which requires that crews of workers walk the lettuce rows, inspecting the heads, thinning any weak head or "doubles" (where two plants are growing in the same spot) and chopping out any weeds.

Thinning and weeding is sufficiently labor intensive that considerable research and development have been undertaken by agencies such as Agricultural Extension and the Agricultural Experiment Station and also by private firms trying to eliminate the process. This R&D was undertaken because attempts were being made by a union and a public agency to eliminate the short-handled hoe (the *cortito*) used for thinning and weeding. Growers argued that the hoe was necessary so that workers would bend closer to the lettuce and inspect it carefully; with the long-handled hoe, such careful inspection, it was argued, was impossible and double heads of lettuce could be missed or weeds tucked under the leaves of the lettuce plant overlooked. Although growers had been searching for means by which the volume of labor could be reduced for thinning and weeding, the elimination after many battles of the short-handled hoe through administrative action of the Department of Industrial Relations of the State of California in 1975 only accelerated attempts by growers to find mechanization or other means to eliminate these operations.

One of the more notable searches for a procedure that will not only eliminate this operation but also increase yields per acre has been undertaken by private development at Bud Antle, the second largest grower-shipper of lettuce in the United States. This process involves greenhouse growing of lettuce seedlings and their transplantation to the fields. More will be said about this process later because it is believed to be a potentially important factor in lettuce harvest mechanization. For now, we should only note that the transplantation process, if it works out well, would eliminate the requirements for thinning and weeding because the lettuce beds can be prepared with herbicides prior to transplantation and because planting is machine controlled so that the problem of doubles is eliminated.

Despite research and development, however, thinning and weeding operations must still be conducted. These are performed by workers external to the lettuce firms, sometimes by the grower-shippers who hire workers on a daily basis or often by specialists in the recruitment and management of temporary workers, for example, labor contractors. This externalized labor force is drawn from three major sources: (1) unskilled workers seeking to develop regular employment but who have not yet done so ("green card" immigrants and undocumented workers); (2) people who are not regularly or continuously in the labor force, particularly housewives; and (3) casual workers who work only as forced to economically. Labor contractors specialize in dealing with these three categories of workers and in bringing them to the workplace. Often the contractors maintain extensive contacts to permit them to draw upon variably sized crews, as weather or other conditions require constant change in the numbers of temporary thinning and weeding workers.

The semiinternalized labor force

This group consists of harvest workers. Originally external in that these workers had no vested rights in any given firm, these workers have developed seniority and other rights ever since the unionization drive started by the United Farm Workers in 1971.[5]

Harvesting activities involve two major kinds and one minor kind of arrangements and therefore involve different kinds of workers and work organization. The most important category of harvest workers, although now in decline, are those involved in the *ground pack* of lettuce – the cutting and packing of naked lettuce into cartons. A second category are those workers involved in the *wrap pack* of lettuce – the cutting and wrapping of lettuce in a plastic film prior to packing it into cartons. Both categories of workers would be severely affected by lettuce harvest mechanization. A third, and minor, arrangement consists of harvesting for shredded lettuce.

Ground pack harvesters

These workers are normally organized into crews that have been, until recently, self-regulating and self-controlled. Crews come in varying sizes, usually consisting of thirty-six workers, although ground pack crew sizes of forty are also reported (Finerman 1974). Most crews are organized with the following workers (Johnson and Zahara 1976b, p. 380):

Select-cut-trim	18
Carton assembly	2
Pack	9
Wash butt (sprayer)	1
Close carton	2
Load	4
Total crew	36

Figures shown do not include supervisors (often two to a crew) or truck drivers (who haul lettuce from the fields).

In the analysis of agricultural labor, ground pack crews constitute one of the most interesting subjects for study. They are probably the most highly paid harvest workers in the United States. Their group incentive system was responsible for the creation of self-regulating and self-reproducing crews until the unionization activities of the early 1970s began to change the system. Although the situation is now in flux, some general characteristics of the ground pack crews include:

1. Crew members are, with few exceptions, of Mexican extraction. Most are probably still Mexican citizens, many being "green-carders" (e.g., legal immigrants to the United States), whereas others are *sindocumentos* (undocumented workers).
2. Many crew members make their permanent home base in Mexico, directly across the border from the Imperial Valley, especially in cities such as Mexicali. An increasing number of workers are probably making their home base in the United States, especially in the Salinas Valley.
3. Crews were, until the early 1970s, almost entirely self-regulated and self-recruited. Grower-shippers, in other words, did not recruit individual workers, assign them to crews, and supervise their work. Rather, workers themselves recruited new crew members as necessary and the crew regulated its own activities, largely determining how much would be produced on a daily basis – dependent, of course, on weather, market, and crop conditions.

The specific mechanisms by which crew members are recruited have not been reported in any scholarly studies nor do we know of any popular materials on this subject.[6]

Crew members were recruited, in the past, through existing members of crews. As a new person was required, an individual crew member could bring a candidate into the crew. The crew member became, in effect, the new person's sponsor and was considered responsible for the work of the candidate. If there were any deficiencies in the work of the new person, that is, an inability to maintain the pace, the sponsor was held responsible for making up the deficiencies. This system of recruitment placed serious obligations on crew members who would not take such responsibilities lightly. Crews work at high speed and sponsors might find themselves paying for their sponsorship through subsidizing a share of the income of the candidates. Sponsorship appears to have been based on (a) kinship, (b) *compadrazco* and related fictive kinship arrangements, and (c) friendship patterns.

4. Crews developed norms for themselves with respect to earnings. In any given crew there is what can be called a "target earnings level" of so many dollars per hour for each crew member. Some crews work much harder than others and therefore earn more. Thus there is a hierarchy of crews in terms of earnings, which establishes the basis for individual movement *between* crews. For movement to occur, however, a receiving crew must have a member willing to become the sponsor of the new individual. Mobility, through this system, consists of individuals initially joining slower crews and then moving into crews with higher target earnings levels. In previous times young individuals could work their way through a hierarchy of crews by developing experience and maintaining their strength. As they got older and were less capable of maintaining the pace, they began to descend the hierarchy.

5. Unionism and its concomitants, especially seniority rights, have begun the process of breaking down the self-recruitment and self-regulation of the crews and initiated the process of internalization of workers into lettuce producing firms. Several processes give rise to these changes. First, unionization tends to encourage restriction on "runaway" piece rates. Unions encourage situations in which earnings levels become homogeneous and regular. Second, the establishment of seniority under union contracts creates the basis for an entirely different crew organization in which workers are assigned to work, and therefore to crews, on the basis of length of individual service rather than on the basis of membership in a crew or the crew's length of service. This process also affects the situation in which crews used to determine their target earnings levels and therefore intercrew mobility. Once intercrew movement declines, the tendency toward homogenization of crew earnings also accelerates.

The key element in the ground pack crews are the "trios," which consist of two cutters and one packer. The cutters move down the rows of lettuce, selecting mature heads, and cutting and trimming them appropriately. Packers follow behind and insert the lettuce heads in the cartons. The top layer is packed with the butts up and the bottom layer with the butts down. The packer leaves the filled carton in the rows. He is followed by a sprayer who sprays the lettuce with water. The cartons are then closed with a hand stapler. With the cartons lying in rows, a truck then moves through them and the cartons are loaded on to the truck. In moving through the fields, the trucks (and any other equipment used) remain in the furrows so that heads left behind will remain undamaged and thereby permit future picking. Normally, a field will be harvested at least two or three times before being sold to a "gunnysacker" (discussed later) or to some other purchaser, or disced under in preparation for new planting.

Wrap pack harvesters

The wrapping of lettuce in a film prior to its sale is a practice found in many areas. In many cases retailers purchase naked lettuce and prepare it on their own premises by trimming damaged or discolored leaves and then wrapping it prior to display and sale. Although there were earlier experiments with wrapping lettuce, the production of lettuce wrapped in the fields, for example, *source-wrapped lettuce,* did not begin seriously until the early 1950s. At that time, with the transition from shed packing to field packing, several experiments were attempted to utilize mobile platforms to facilitate the packing of naked lettuce. These experiments failed because the slowest packer on the platforms controlled the pace of all the packers on the machine.

A major problem involved in developing the technique of wrapping lettuce depended on the quality of the film for wrapping. Initial experiments proved unsatisfactory but once this problem was resolved, several companies moved rapidly into the wrapping of lettuce, adapting the movable platforms that had been experimented with earlier.

Film wrapping was an immediate success and then nearly as quickly a failure. One company was reported to be shipping 15 to 20 percent almost immediately on the development of the technique but this dropped to 5 percent by 1964 (Padfield and Martin 1965, p. 67). The reason for the vagaries concerned the initial attractiveness of wrapped lettuce to retailers (because it saved the costs of trimming and wrapping in urban areas with their higher labor costs as well as the elimination of costs of removal of

Table 3.6. *Comparison of Wrap Crew Production Organization*

Padfield and Martin		Johnson and Zahara	
Number in crews	Wrap crews	Number in crews	Wrap crews
10–12	Cutters	14	Select-cut-trim
4	Setup men (lift the lettuce to the machine	1	Carton assembler
6	Wrappers	9	Wrappers
3	Packers	4	Packers
1	Gluer	2	Closers
1	Stitcher-driver		
2	Loaders	3	Loaders
27–29	Total	33	Total

trimmed material as garbage) and the quick discovery that, unless high quality lettuce was packed carefully, rates of deterioration and costs of unwrapping and trimming lettuce could skyrocket total costs. Accordingly, wrapped lettuce declined in sales but there has been slow and steady recapture of this segment of the lettuce market since the 1960s.

At present, wrapped lettuce constitutes approximately 20 percent or more of the lettuce production (Drossler 1976, p. 48), although there are indications that, in several of the larger lettuce firms, 40 to 50 percent of production is shipped source wrapped to the east coast. It is generally anticipated in the industry that the percentage of wrapped lettuce will continue to increase; because of cost savings, retailers indicate a preference for it. (Drossler 1976, p. 58). The latest study, the Drossler Report, estimates that 54 percent of all lettuce may be source wrapped by 1980 (Drossler 1976, p. 60).

Basic technology and crew organization in the production of source-wrapped lettuce has changed only slightly since the development of the technique in the 1950s. One way to compare the production organization is to examine the wrap crews studied by Padfield and Martin (1965, pp. 58–9) with those studied by Johnson and Zahara (1976, p. 380) (see Table 3.6).

No studies have yet been published on the character of wrapped-lettuce crews so that inferences about their characteristics can only be made from fragmentary evidence.[7] The characteristics of these crews appear to differ substantially from the ground pack crews.

1. Wrapped-lettuce crews contain a significant proportion of women, unlike naked-lettuce crews. Although the number of women varies from crew to crew and from employer to employer, some wrap crews have been observed in which women did all of the wrapping and a great deal of the cutting. On the other hand, women rarely seem to pack lettuce into cartons.
2. Unlike ground pack workers, wrap crews appear to be heavily composed of people who live in the area in which the lettuce is growing and being harvested. Thus, unlike the ground pack workers, fewer of these workers "follow the loop" of lettuce production, although apparently some do.
3. Wrap crews on the whole do not operate under an incentive system, either individual or group. Paid on an hourly basis, they have much less incentive for the type of output found among ground pack crews. Supervision, as a consequence, is external with employers staffing the wrap machines with supervisory personnel who function more as "pushers" than as quality controllers, as is the case with ground pack crews.
4. Crew members are heavily of Mexican background but probably have fewer Mexican nationals than can be found in the ground pack crews. Wrap crews are also more heterogeneous: It is unusual to find a ground pack crew that is not ethnically homogeneous, whereas wrap crews may have Anglos or Blacks, although in small numbers.
5. For many wrap crew workers, working in lettuce is not a full-time, year-round occupation, and therefore they are less involved in activities surrounding lettuce production. Thus although many wrap crew workers joined unions during the upsurge of union organizing in 1971, wrapping workers were less prominent and active in union activities.

Shredded-lettuce harvesters

Shredded lettuce is known in the trade by several names, including "precut" and "processed" lettuce. In this form lettuce is prepared by cutting and shredding the lettuce heads; to the lettuce mixture other vegetables such as carrots and red cabbage may be added. Typically, shredded lettuce is used by institutional users, hospitals, schools, prisons, and the like, which do not wish to prepare whole lettuce heads into salads. As previously noted, the market for shredded lettuce is increasing, less because of traditional institutional usage but more because of the growth of fast-food, and franchised-food operations such as McDonald's, Denny's, or Sambo's.

In previous times, shredded lettuce was prepared by specialist firms, which purchased naked lettuce and prepared it for local sale. A common phenomenon, particularly in the West, was the "gunnysacker," a firm that would purchase a field of lettuce after several regular harvests to glean whatever lettuce heads remained. Gunnysackers might sell the lettuce in bulk to shredders or occasionally shred the lettuce themselves for sale.

Recently, the market for shredded lettuce has increased to the point that significant changes appear to be in the offing. Perhaps one of the most important is the entry of Bud Antle, Inc. into shredded-lettuce production. Antle, the second largest lettuce grower-shipper, has developed a movable configuration of equipment specially geared to lettuce shredding. The equipment consists of specially designed trucks and several trailers that contain shredding, washing, cooling, and spinning facilities. The Antle process involves the utilization of trucks geared to move at highway speeds as well as at speeds appropriate to harvesting. The trucks carry their own conveyors, which carry the lettuce in bucket-type arrangements. Covering ten rows, between eight to ten harvesters walk the rows behind the conveyor, cutting the lettuce, removing their cores, and positioning them in the buckets. The lettuce is conveyed to storage inside the truck, which when loaded is driven to the processing station. Here the lettuce is conveyed into the trailers where it is shredded, cooled and washed, and then spun dry in a centrifuge. The lettuce is then hand packed in ten-pound plastic bags and placed in cartons. Next, it is transported to cooling rooms and moved into transportation as necessary (Franta 1975). With tight control over temperature at all times, shredded lettuce is expected to have a shelf life of fourteen days. The Antle firm airfreights this product to places as far as Hong Kong and Germany.

Although Antle is the only major grower-shipper currently producing shredded lettuce, tendencies toward increase in its production are noticeable. One gunnysacker has improved the process of harvest and handling of lettuce over previous technologies (Linden 1977a). His technique involves the harvest of lettuce in bulk bins and their shipment to shredding firms throughout the country. Another development involves the conjunction of Michigan and Florida lettuce growers (Hagar 1977). In this case a Michigan grower has begun a shredding operation that draws lettuce from its associated Florida firm after the Michigan season has closed. Both firms shred lettuce and sell it to buyers in their region. In one month, when Michigan lettuce is unavailable and Florida lettuce is not yet mature, California lettuce must be purchased on the market, otherwise both firms are self-sufficient producers.

Lettuce shredding is more capital intensive than other forms of lettuce production. Labor is used primarily for harvesting and to a limited degree in processing the lettuce. Were the market for shredded lettuce to increase significantly, it could potentially fit together with harvest mechanization because the major labor input, at present, is in cutting, trimming, and coring the lettuce. Although attempts at marketing shredded lettuce to retailers have been undertaken, it is anticipated that the increase in the market for shredded lettuce will come primarily from institutional users. Thus shredded lettuce can be considered as one possible contributor to lettuce harvest mechanization, but it is unlikely that its contributions will be more significant than the other forms of lettuce production.

It was not always thus

The relatively brief description of how lettuce is currently produced does not provide much insight into the evolution of the present system of lettuce production. We turn now to a brief examination of the history of lettuce production to illuminate the present production process.

The earliest forms of harvesting involved naked lettuce. This process evolved during the 1920s and consisted of moving sizable crews of relatively unskilled workers to cut lettuce and throw the heads into large bins, which were hauled through the fields. Cutters were mainly ethnic minorities, especially Mexicans and Filipinos. From the fields, the bins were hauled to packing sheds, which were built in the various lettuce districts. Some sheds were built by growers as they enlarged and became grower-shippers, whereas others were built by ice companies and/or railway companies. In the early days there was much greater capacity for packing than was actually used.

Inside the sheds the lettuce was trimmed and then packed into wooden crates. The lettuce was iced by hand before the crates were closed. The crates were moved on roller conveyors to the railway cars ("reefers") in which they were stacked by hand. The packing sheds constituted a sizable capital investment for their builders because they involved a variety of handling equipment, including conveyors, freezing units to make ice, ice shredders, conveyors for moving the shredded ice, and so on. At a rather early stage, lettuce packing inside the sheds became an occupation occupied almost entirely by Anglos. By the 1940s, in any case, lettuce production was notably stratified, with field labor being increasingly of Mexican extraction and shed labor being almost entirely Anglo.

Unionism was notable by its presence in the sheds and absence in the fields. The struggle for unionization was continuous, with major strikes occurring after 1928 (Lamb 1942, Chapter 8; Watson 1977). By the end of the 1940s unions were fairly well established in the sheds but not in the fields. The introduction of vacuum cooling early in the 1950s gave growers the opportunity to utilize technological change to provide a cheaper, although more labor-extensive, system of lettuce harvesting. Vacuum cooling involves the chilling of lettuce in large tubes from which air is removed; the removal of air chills the lettuce more rapidly than can be accomplished through icing it directly. The vacuum process represented a decline in capital intensivity because the vacuum tubes demanded less capital than the sheds and their ice-making equipment.

Vacuum cooling also permitted a shift from packing the lettuce in sheds to packing it in the fields. Field labor was cheaper than shed labor not only because it was nonunionized but also because it was available in considerable supply through the continuous migration of Mexicans to the United States. Indeed, during and after World War II, movement of Mexicans was organized intergovernmentally and formalized in 1951 with the adoption of Public Law 78 (Galarza 1964, p. 51). An additional factor that played a role in the shift was that shed workers were covered by the National Labor Relations Act, whereas field-workers in agriculture were excluded; accordingly, once packing was moved to the fields, the shed workers' union began to atrophy. Although this union, Local 78, still exists, it is only a fragment of what it had been (Watson 1977).

The vacuum-cooling process thus facilitated a shift from shed to field packing, from Anglo to Mexican workers, and was significantly responsible for undermining existing unions in agriculture (Smith 1961; Glass 1966). The use of *braceros,* however, meant that additional changes had to be made. For one thing, the old wooden crate had to be abandoned for a container that would handle a smaller weight of lettuce; in the packing sheds, the extensive use of conveyors facilitated the use of large containers; in the fields, smaller containers had to be used because conveyors were not available. This resulted in the introduction of the present fiberboard carton, which holds between 45–65 pounds of lettuce. More important, a new category of workers had to be trained for the skills necessary to pack lettuce. Whereas braceros had been used earlier simply as cutters and needed to know only whether or not the lettuce was mature, now they had to learn how to pack lettuce into the cartons. The new skills involved not only recognizing the mature head but cutting and trimming it appropriately, leaving a number of "wrapper leaves," which protected the lettuce in transit, positioning it appropriately in the box and obtaining the proper "squeeze" so that the heads were packed neither too tightly nor too loosely.

Originally, field-workers were paid on an hourly basis but at some point they began to be paid on a piece-work basis. Over time, the group incentive system that now characterizes naked-lettuce harvesting emerged.

As the bracero program came under increasing criticism, grower-shippers of lettuce, and California growers generally, became increasingly concerned about the maintenance of their supply of labor. Two basic actions were undertaken: (1) growers "hedged their bets" about the labor supply by encouraging research in mechanization of the harvest; and (2) growers began to explore means to convert their former braceros into legal immigrants to the United States. In the first case, research was encouraged and supported at the University of California, Davis, where Professor Roger Garrett developed the first prototype lettuce harvester. However, the new machine was not necessary because the second strategy developed by the growers was successful. This involved the conversion of the bracero lettuce harvesters into "normal" U.S.-based workers through a process of obtaining green cards for them. The character of this shift, from braceros to green-carders, has never been described anywhere despite the fact that it occurred not only in lettuce but in other commodities, although to a lesser degree. The probabilities are that lettuce growers became sponsors of braceros as immigrants, selecting braceros who had demonstrated reliability in their work and encouraging them to apply for immigrant status.

By 1966 the transition from braceros to green-carders was apparently complete and the present form of crew organization had emerged. One of the consequences of the transition from bracero to green card was apparently a reduction in the size of the harvest crew. Padfield and Martin (1965) describe crew size in 1963, during the bracero period, as involving in the case of "G Company," eighty-five to eighty-six workers. These included:

40	Cutter-trimmers
20	Packers
6	Closers
4	Water boys
3–4	Box spreaders

6	Windrower-loaders
1	Stacker or folder
1	Stitcher-driver
2	Pushers or row bosses
1	Foreman

Padfield and Martin report that ground crews were usually composed of sixty nationals who cut and packed exclusively while about sixteen local people filled the remaining positions. In the Red Rock harvest, which they observed directly, there were eighty nationals (Mexicans) in each ground crew "to allow for the fluctuations in the number of locals" (Padfield and Martin 1965, p. 57).

"H Company," as reported by Padfield and Martin, had a crew of seventy-nine workers that included fifty-four nationals and twenty-five locals. This crew consisted of:

36	Cutter-trimmers
18	Packers
3	Water boys
6	Closers
3–4	Box spreaders
2–3	Windrowers
4	Loaders
1	Stacker or folder
1	Stitcher or driver
3	Row bosses
1	Foreman

There are some similarities between the crews as studied by Padfield and Martin in 1963 and present-day crews as well as some significant differences. The basic size of the crew was much larger, and the presence of locals (Americans), in contrast to the present crews that are constituted almost entirely of Mexicans, is notable. At the same time, the basic relationship of two cutter-trimmers to one packer was already established. About the only non-Mexicans present in the crews nowadays are supervisory employees such as field bosses; row bosses, however, who provide immediate supervision to the crews, tend to be of Mexican origin.

There are a small number of crews made up of Filipinos in lettuce harvesting but the overwhelming bulk of harvesters are Mexican nationals. Occasional individuals of other origin, for example, Blacks, perhaps occasionally an Anglo, turn up in auxiliary activities to the crew, but rarely as cutter-trimmers or packers.

The similarities between crews, other than in total size, between the early 1950s and the present, is not really surprising because the basic technology involved in harvesting has remained unchanged since that time. In the early 1950s the transition to vacuum cooling, carton packing (vs. crate packing), and field packing (vs. shed packing), constituted the last major technological development in lettuce harvesting. Since then, a great many small-scale innovations have occurred, but the basic process has remained untouched. Accordingly, it is reasonable to anticipate that the basic organization of the harvesting crews would remain the same.

How many lettuce workers are there?

The number of workers employed in lettuce production constitutes a major mystery, which is partially a function of the confidentiality that lettuce grower-shippers maintain with respect to information about their operations. In a highly competitive production system grower-shippers have been notably reluctant to indicate the size of their operations, their volume of sales, or other information. Nothing is known, therefore, about the numbers of workers employed by different firms nor about the numbers of different types of workers.

In this section we will examine various data sources, compare figures, and develop our own estimate of the probable number of *harvest* workers involved. These workers not only constitute the bulk of people employed in the lettuce production but the data sources about them are most voluminous. The number of workers employed in preharvest operations is not only more difficult to estimate but many preharvest workers are casual and part time. The numbers of workers employed in shredded lettuce is sufficiently small, at the moment, to permit their being overlooked. These omissions, however, provide significant problems: In preparing for the social consequences of a transition to mechanized harvesting, it would be appropriate for the public agencies involved to have an acute sense of the total numbers of workers to be affected.

Employment Development Department sources

The major source about the number of lettuce workers in California is the Employment Development Department (EDD) of the state of California. This administrative agency has had various names in times past (e.g., Human Resources Development) and currently houses antecedent government agencies such as the Employment Service and the Rural Manpower Service.[8]

The problems that develop with utilization of EDD data are manifold despite the fact that EDD publishes the most voluminous data. These data are significant, however, for their unsatisfactory basis. The following problems are involved in using EDD sources:

1. The numbers of workers working are based neither on a head count of actual numbers on any given day of work nor on an inventory of actual workers by name. Instead, the numbers are synthesized from labor requirements per acre (or other unit) of production. Thus when EDD reports in its Form 881-A on "Numbers Working," this is not a reflection of any social reality but a synthesis of numbers based on economic and/or time studies of labor inputs.

2. The "numbers working" are rarely reported by consistent types of activities. In lettuce, for example, four major categories are utilized to report on different types of work activities. These include: PCH (plant-cultivate-harvest); preharvest; harvest; and thin-hoe-harvest. Because different categories are used to report by county, it is impossible to assemble data even within a distinct production district by type of activity. For example, the Salinas Valley constitutes a single production district for which reports are made with respect to the shipments of lettuce. This production district is composed of three counties. In two counties, Monterey and San Benito, the categories used to report are preharvest and harvest. In the other county, Santa Cruz, the single reporting category is PCH. This method of reporting makes it impossible to develop any sense, even through the use of synthetic data, of the numbers of workers involved in a given activity. Because different kinds of workers are used in both preharvest and harvest activities, the fact that they are being lumped together obscures the numbers found in each type of activity.

Further problems can be seen when examining the actual data sources provided through EDD. Table 3.7, for example, has been drawn from the *California Annual Farm Labor Report* for the years 1965–72. The figures provided are given for "lettuce" without the type of activity being specified.

Table 3.8, by contrast, is drawn from EDD's Bulletin 881-A, a report issued at different time intervals, initially weekly, but currently semimonthly. Bulletin 881-A provides data by county and types of activities. County data have been grouped by production district in the table for 1972. The variation by time period, according to the season, in numbers of workers employed can be seen to be considerable. One way to subsume the variation is to take the number of workers employed during the peaks of two production seasons – in January during the winter produc-

Table 3.7. *Peak Employment, Lettuce Workers, California, 1964–1972*

Year	Peak Employed
1964	8,500
1965	6,230
1966	5,470
1967	5,400
1968	6,170
1969	6,260
1970	5,620
1971	5,510
1972	6,610

Source: California, *Annual Farm Labor Reports,* 1964–72.

Table 3.8. *Peak Season Employment, Salinas–Imperial, 1969–77*

Year	Salinas District	Imperial Valley
1969	4,130	4,240
1970	4,640	4,240
1971	4,460	3,000
1972	5,130	3,650
1973	4,940	3,950
1974	5,120	4,850
1975	6,000	5,150
1976	5,570	5,300

Imperial figures are for the winter season, October of previous year to April of year showing.
Source: Employment Development Department, Form 881-A.

tion period and in June, at the peak of the Salinas Valley season. These data are reported in Table 3.8.

Other data sources

Data on the number of workers are also provided through other sources. Johnson and Zahara (1976b, p. 380), for example, report: "From correspondence with county sources, total full-time crew equivalents are estimated to range from 105 to 170, with an average of 130 crews during the 1974–75 crop season." Later in their report, Johnson and Zahara assume the existence of "100 ground pack crews and 30 wrap crews in California and Arizona" in order to develop the calculations necessary for their work.

If we accept the data provided by Johnson and Zahara (1976b), it would provide an estimate of between 3,465 and 6,120 workers, based on an assumption of 105 crews of 33 workers (as the low) and 170 crews of 36 workers (as the high). If, in contrast, we utilize the figures that Johnson and Zahara provide of their estimates, for example, 100 ground pack crews and 30 wrap crews in California and Arizona, with 36 workers in each ground pack crew and 33 workers in the wrap crews, a total of 4,590 harvest workers is yielded.

The unsatisfactory character of the Johnson–Zahara estimates is revealed when we calculate what production might result from their crew estimates when multiplied by productivity and number of hours estimated to be worked each year:

Ground pack crews:

> 560 cartons/hour × 2,240 hours/year × 100 crews
> = 125,440,000 cartons

Wrap crews:

> 178 cartons/hour × 2,240 hours/year × 30 crews = 11,961,700 cartons

Total production:

> 125,440,000 + 11,901,600 = 137,401,600 cartons

Because annual production in 1974 was 98,353,000 cartons in California and Arizona, the unsatisfactory basis for calculations is clear.

Another way to synthesize data on the number of workers is to take production figures and productivity data and develop them together. Thus, in 1976, total production of lettuce from California and Arizona was 105,138,000 cartons (Federal-State Market News Service 1976, Table 1). Let us assume that there were 21,027,600 cartons of wrapped lettuce and 84,110,400 cartons of ground-packed lettuce (based on production being 20 percent wrapped and 80 percent ground packed). Johnson and Zahara (1976b, Table 2, p. 380) report crew output at 560 cartons per hour for ground pack and 178 cartons per hour in wrap pack. We further assume that crews work, on the average, 40 hours per week and 45 weeks during the year; this equals a work year of 1,800 hours (which we consider much more realistic than the 2,240 hours assumed by Johnson and Zahara). Based on these data, we develop the following calculations:

Wrap-packed lettuce:

$$\frac{21{,}027{,}600 \text{ cartons}}{178 \text{ cartons / hour}} = 188{,}133 \text{ hours}$$

$$\frac{118{,}133}{1800} = 65.6 \text{ crews}$$

$$66 \text{ crews} \times 33 \text{ workers} = 2178 \text{ wrap pack workers}$$

Ground-packed lettuce:

$$\frac{84{,}110{,}400 \text{ cartons}}{560 \text{ cartons / hour}} = 150{,}197 \text{ hours}$$

$$\frac{150{,}197}{1800} = 83.4 \text{ crews}$$

$$84 \text{ crews} \times 36 \text{ workers} = 3{,}024 \text{ workers}$$

$$2{,}178 + 3{,}024 = 5{,}202 \text{ workers,}$$
or more accurately,
job opportunities.

This estimate will be seen to be 13 percent higher than the total number of workers estimated by Johnson and Zahara.

Our own estimates place the number of actual workers somewhat higher than either the Johnson and Zahara figures or the preceding 5,202 synthesized figure. We base this on our belief that the number of workers actually employed in lettuce harvesting is higher than what might be calculated through any synthesis based on working hours, productivity, or numbers of crews, although the number of crews may be fairly accurate (because the margin of estimate is sizeable, e.g., 105–170). Interviews with lettuce workers as well as some observations indicate that all lettuce crews experience considerable absenteeism from day to day as well as turnover. Our observations, therefore, indicate that a figure between 6,000 and 7,500 actual lettuce workers is more realistic, accounting for the absenteeism that we believe occurs. These figures constitute what we believe is the actual numbers of people working, not the number of "equivalents." We estimate that about 60 percent of the workers are employed in ground pack and 40 percent in wrap pack. Thus our estimate of the number of workers is:

3,600–4,500   Ground pack harvesters
2,400–3,000   Wrap pack harvesters

These figures will provide the basis for our assumptions in Chapter 4 when we estimate the impact of lettuce harvest mechanization.

Grower organization as a factor in the lettuce system

Whereas labor constitutes a vital factor that would be affected by harvest mechanization and, consequently, one to which we have devoted considerable attention, lettuce growers constitute a second crucial element with which we must be concerned. Unlike workers, however, who are affected by changes in a production and distribution system, lettuce growers are primarily those who produce the change because they are the ones who make decisions with respect to the implementation of technology. Yet proposed lettuce harvest mechanization and other technological changes, discussed in the next chapter, will also affect growers.

The main points this section will develop are that (1) growers constitute a distinctive and organized segment of the lettuce production and distribution system, and (2) their organizational capacities, however, are limited by their abilities to agree with respect to external factors relating to the industry but a limited ability to agree on internal elements. Thus we will argue that the growers have shown remarkable capacity for utilizing organization as a tool or weapon.[9] However, this capacity to organize has not been translatable into a capacity to regulate internal relationships, particularly with respect to production, because of three factors: (1) the inelasticity of demand for lettuce and the inability of growers, until the present, to affect demand; (2) the manner in which the market is organized that permits domination of the lettuce market by large lettuce purchasers, especially supermarket chains; and (3) the sheer numbers of growers and other agencies involved (sales agencies, brokers, agents, etc.), all of which affect the capacity of the industry to regulate production internally.

Grower-shippers as individual firms

Grower-shippers come in different sizes and types. Table 3.3 provides one picture of the different handling firms according to the volume shipped. Table 3.9 shows the size of individual growing-shipping organizations in 1976 according to volume of carlots shipped.

Table 3.9. *Carlots Shipped by Individual Firms*

Antle	16,800	Western Packing	800
Church	7,500	Kelly	750
Pacific Lettuce	7,000	Mission Packing	750
Finerman	6,400	Minami	728
D'Arrigo Bros.	5,500	Fudenna	700
Furukawa	5,000	Pacific Produce	700
Admiral	4,200	Eckel	700
Growers Exchange	3,450	Harden	700
Norton	3,300	Pepelis	600
Mills	3,000	Bodine	600
J. A. Wood	2,855	Sahara	575
Englund	2,700	Arakelian	500
Mapes	2,500	Point Sal	500
Samsel	2,350	Mazzie	500
Andrews Sons	2,250	Singh	500
Salinas Marketing	2,000	Fisher Ranch	500
Green Valley	2,000	Woods Co.	500
Mendelson-Zeller	2,000	California Lettuce	500
Sears-Schumann	2,000	Koyama	500
Saikhon	2,000	Graeser-Pepelis	475
Merrill	1,900	Walsh	425
Turner	1,582	Sakata	420
Byrd	1,500	Consaul	400
Senini	1,500	Cactus	350
Salinas Lettuce	1,500	Suzy-Bel	300
Baillie	1,400	Century	300
Martori Brothers	1,350	Nish Noroian	300
Bonita	1,317	J & A Farms	300
Maggio	1,300	Williams	250
Vessey & Co.	1,200	L & J	250
Merit	1,129	Pilibos	250
Del Mar	1,100	Apache	250
Santa Clara	1,000	Pandol	200
Abatti	1,000	Western Growers	200
Nunes Company	1,000	Oshita	191
Let-Us-Pak	1,000	Mettler	180
Danenberg	1,000	Oceano	100
Arrow	1,000	Yo Katayama	50
Donovan	1,000	Pam Pak	50
Pacific Farm	935	Bradley	20
J-B Distributing	900	B & C	11
Pleasant Valley	800	Sunnyside	5
Colace	800		

Source: Packer Availability and Merchandising Guide and the *Redbook*, Spring 1976, (Vance Publishing Corporation, Chicago).

Two points must immediately be made about the table: First, the table shows total carlots of all commodities (not just lettuce) shipped; second, a number of firms, including what was probably at the time the largest in the industry, Inter Harvest,[10] do not provide information on the number of carlots shipped. Hence the table must be treated, as must all such data, as indicative rather than as definitive.

Lettuce production organizations can be subsumed in three basic ways: (1) size, (2) character of production, and (3) corporate organization. Thus lettuce producers come in a variety of sizes and some have larger shares of the market than others. By examining the data collected by the federal government in 1969 of the purchase of a number of lettuce producers by United Brands (Federal Trade Commission 1976), it is feasible to get some idea of the dominance of a number of firms. Data produced on this occasion, although not organized to permit a systematic analysis of the relative size of grower-shippers, demonstrates the fact that in creating Inter Harvest as a subsidiary of United Brands, a single firm that would be the largest in the industry was being created. Table 3.9 provides additional data on size. In addition, it is generally known in the industry that three single firms, Sun Harvest, Bud Antle, and Bruce Church, each handles about 10 percent of California–Arizona production. The firm of Mel Finerman probably also comes close to handling an additional 10 percent.[11] Furthermore, although no data are available, it is commonly known that the Garin Company constitutes another sizable firm.

In addition to size, firms also differ in types of production. Although most lettuce growers also grow and harvest a number of other commodities such as celery, broccoli, and cauliflower, these crops are represented in different volumes and importance for some growers. In addition, some, too, grow crops such as asparagus that are not grown by other growers. Antle, for example, grew pecans in Arizona as part of their production package. For many, but not all individual firms, lettuce constitutes the most important crop; it is the money-maker but can also be the money loser. Grower-shippers do not report on the relative importance of lettuce and other crops, so that it is possible to form only some impressions on this matter. However, there is little doubt that lettuce is more central for some production organizations than for others.

One factor that differentiates lettuce production organizations is whether they own land or develop other relationships to obtain use of the land on which lettuce is grown. For example, some of the smaller growing-shipping organizations in the Salinas Valley own land there whereas some of the larger firms do not – either leasing their land or working joint ventures with land owner-growers. On the whole, our impression is that the larger firms are less inclined to own land than the smaller ones are.

An additional factor differentiating lettuce grower-shippers is their form of organization and relationship to other entities. Here we can distinguish two basic types of firms, the second with two basic subtypes:

1. Corporate subsidiaries
2. Independents
   a. Corporations
   b. Cooperatives

At the moment there are few corporate subsidiaries in lettuce production. The main one in existence is Sun Harvest, originally formed under the name Inter Harvest, a subsidiary of United Brands (formerly the United Fruit Company), which purchased a number of lettuce firms in 1969 and integrated them into a single organization. It fought the attempts of the federal government to prevent the purchase, and has successfully conducted business since.

Around the same time as the creation of Inter Harvest, another large corporate conglomerate, Purex, purchased a number of lettuce and other producers with the intention of developing a lettuce production subsidiary. Purex sold off its purchases when, among other things, it was threatened by a boycott of Purex products by the United Farm Workers Union (UFW) in 1971. In contrast, Inter Harvest signed a contract with the UFW, thereby avoiding boycotts on its Chiquita label (associated with bananas). In 1978 Bud Antle was acquired by Castle and Cooke, the large multinational food production organization (Dole pineapple, Bumble Bee tuna and salmon, and other products). The indications are that large multinational corporate entities are manifesting some interest in acquiring well-established lettuce firms. At the same time, the hazardous character of lettuce pricing causes hesitations. If grower organizations were to become firmer with respect to production controls (discussed further later), there is the possibility of increased interest in the acquisition of established production organizations by larger entities, which would then use their acquired firms as subsidiaries.

Independent lettuce producers come in a variety of sizes but the tendency is for these firms to be smaller. Excepting a few major producers such as Bruce Church, most of the independents are smaller in production volume. These independents are distinctive firms that were established by risk-taking individuals who dealt with lettuce as produce merchants, sales agents, and the like, rather than actual producers.[12]

In contrast to the independent firms are the cooperatives such as the Salinas Lettuce Farmers Cooperative, the Salinas Marketing Cooperative, and the Green Valley Produce Co-op. Composed of smaller producers, these firms survive because their aggregated production volume positions them to compete with the moderate-sized grower-shippers.

One additional factor about lettuce producers is that the larger firms operate in California and Arizona, in a variety of districts, to produce and sell lettuce every week of the year. Firms such as Sun Harvest, Bud Antle, Bruce Church, and Garin produce in Salinas during the spring, summer, and fall seasons and then move through a regular cycle to the central San Joaquin Valley for a short season prior to beginning winter production in the Imperial Valley and Palo Verde (Riverside County in California) areas and/or in various production districts in Arizona. The larger firms also have a short production season in the early spring in the southern San Joaquin Valley area prior to the beginning of the Salinas Valley spring season. Many of the smaller growing-shipping organizations follow part *but not all* of this cycle, perhaps skipping a portion of the season in the San Joaquin Valley. In contrast, some firms ship only from the Imperial Valley (or some other winter district) but do not produce lettuce on a year-round basis.

In addition to the geographic dispersion between the two major production districts, Salinas and Imperial, we must note the important Santa Maria district comprising the counties of San Luis Obispo, Santa Barbara and Ventura. The Santa Maria district is peculiar because it was a production area geared for a long time toward the southern California market. It was believed that Santa Maria lettuce was not of sufficiently high quality so that it could be shipped nationally. In recent years, however, Santa Maria lettuce has been entering into the national market. Santa Maria producers tend to be smaller than those found in the Salinas–Imperial production areas and often are heavily involved with the production of crops other than lettuce (e.g., the firm of H. Y. Minami and Sons is a major producer of strawberries as well as of lettuce; see *Packer* 1977a, pp. 110, 195).

Perhaps one way to gain a better "feel" for the character of lettuce grower-shippers is to take one firm, Bud Antle, and to describe it in some detail. The Antle firm prides itself as being the "maverick" of the industry[13] and has been one of the major technological innovators in lettuce production. In this sense it is hardly typical of the industry, but an examination of the firm will provide a better sense of what individual lettuce-producing organizations are like.[14]

Bud Antle began in the lettuce business by creating a firm based in Watsonville in 1943. In 1949, when experimentation with vacuum cooling began, Antle was one of the first to innovate. In 1953 Antle and Church established a subsidiary organization, the Vacuum Cooling Corporation, which later sold the patents on the process, obtained after extensive negotiations and litigation, to an industry-created organization. Beginning in 1960 Antle experimented with film wrapping of lettuce; at this time Antle apparently began an association with the Dow Chemical Company, a subsidiary of which provided the film for wrapping the lettuce. This association later involved the sale of Antle land to Dow, which then also became a stockholder in the Antle Company.

On May 1, 1961 Antle proved his maverick quality by signing a contract covering field-workers with the Teamsters Union. This act so enraged other growers that Antle was expelled from the California Council of Growers and had to resign from the Grower-Shipper Vegetable Association. The contract with the Teamsters has never been fully explained, although it is believed by many sources that Antle signed because his firm was in financial difficulties and the Teamsters made pension funds available to him on an investment basis with the "price" being a contract covering the field-workers (see the *Salinas Californian,* March 30, 1963; April 2, 1963).

Bud Antle Inc. also maintained a subsidiary, the House of Bud, "formed to operate outlets in the terminal markets of New York, Philadelphia, Pittsburgh, Boston, and Puerto Rico for the wholesale distribution of the Company's products as well as fresh fruits and vegetables grown and shipped by others" (Antle 1972, p. 14). The House of Bud in turn had a subsidiary to market Dominican bananas (Antle 1972, p. 14). The parent firm, Bud Antle Inc., leased a fleet of piggyback trucks for shipping produce and owned land and support facilities including vacuum coolers at Watsonville, Holtville (in the Imperial Valley), and Red Rock (Arizona). Most land, according to the prospectus, that was in ownership was to provide space for support facilities and "substantially" all farming was done on leased land (Antle, 1972, p. 18). Molding plants were also maintained at Salinas and Holtville, to provide for polystyrene containers used to ship celery.

Other sources (Mackintosh 1977, pp. 286–7; Lappé and Collins 1979, pp. 286–8) inform us that the House of Bud had a European organization based in Brussels, Belgium. According to these sources, the House of Bud formed a subsidiary in turn known as *Bud Senegal,* after one of the House of Bud officers noted the similarities between geophysical conditions in Senegal and the Imperial Valley. Bud Senegal received financial support from the Senegalese government to begin growing fresh produce intended for air shipment to the European market. Little is known about the operations of Bud Senegal or the House of Bud's European operations but Bud Senegal has been nationalized by the Senegalese government with financial arrangements beneficial to the House of Bud. At the same time, similar rumors hold that the House of Bud has begun operations in a number of other African countries bordering on the southern Sahara where geophysical conditions are proximate to those found in the Imperial Valley.

Bud Antle, Inc., at the time of the publication of its stock prospectus, was essentially a family-owned organization. The head of the company in 1972 was Bob Antle, Bud's son. Family members, including Bud's divorced wife, two sons, and one married daughter originally owned 1,705,554 shares, or 90.16 percent of the total of 1,891,609 shares in the company. The only sizable shareholder in the company prior to the publication of the prospectus was the Dow Chemcial Investment and Finance Corporation holding 133,333 shares, or 6.9 percent, of total shareholdings. The stock prospectus intended to offer shares of stock for sale to the public, after which family holdings would be reduced to 68.36 percent of total stockholdings.

The innovative character of Antle as an organization can be seen not only historically in terms of Antle's early involvement with vacuum cooling, film wrapping, and labor contracts, but also in current technological developments. Antle has been experimenting directly with mechanized harvesting of lettuce; other lettuce firms tend to look ot other sources, particularly the Agricultural Research Service of the U.S. Department of Agriculture, for research and development. Similarly, Antle has introduced a new system for the palletization of lettuce and is experimenting with the development of a seedlings system for planting; both will be described later in this chapter.

Although the Antle organization is unusual among lettuce producers by way of being "maverick," the family basis for organization of these large-scale producers is not unusual. We have already noted the Finerman company, which traces its origins to a single individual, Mel Finerman. Finerman (1974) informs us that the main stockholders in this company were Finerman, Marshall Davis (executive vice-president and vice-chairman), and Leo Goldberg (secretary-treasurer and vice-chairman). Minor stockholders were Alfred P. Carpenter (president of Finerman) and Jerry Goldstine (senior vice-president).

Although less information is available about them, it is known that principal figures in a number of other lettuce firms are family members. Thus Tom Church is sales manager of Bruce Church, Inc. (Linden 1977b), Tom Merrill heads up Merrill Farms, and Paul Englund is involved with the R. T. Englund Company.

Individuals engaged in lettuce production, particularly family members and top operating officers of the companies, constitute an informal community highly involved with each other. Like the occupational community of printers described by Lipset et al. (1956), the continual movement of lettuce production and the special character of its daily sale help to create a sense of special community of interest. Lettuce growers express this community through a tendency toward social closure; they are at one and the same time competitors with each other in sales, yet close to one another in experiencing the same life conditions that separate them from other groups. Similar to Lipset's printers whose working hours set them apart from other occupations and whose specialized skills requiring high literacy distinguished them from other manual workers despite the manual character of their labor, lettuce grower-shippers are separated from other growers by the peripatetic character of production and the unique qualities of lettuce as a market crop.

The character of the informal community has contributed to the development of grower organizations, to which we now turn.

Grower organizations

Grower organizations, it should be noted at the outset, although often focused upon lettuce growers, are not necessarily limited to firms that specialize in lettuce. The formation of organizations by growers in California and throughout the United States is notable. Lettuce growers constitute one definite grouping that tends to be concentrated in distinctive organizations that lettuce growers dominate while they may also be dispersed in a great many other organizations of growers.

Lettuce growers are organized into two basic types of organizations: permanent integrative organizations and temporary special-purpose organizations. Of the first type, the most notable is the Western Growers and Shippers Association. This is an organization in which lettuce growers predominate but which also includes growers of other commodities as well as a host of associated members related to the production of fresh commodities but not actual growers; it also includes the grower-shipper associations of a number of producing districts, particularly the

Salinas, Imperial, Oxnard, and Yuma areas. In addition to these organizations, there are others such as the Central California Lettuce Producers Cooperative, an organization created in an attempt to develop more orderly marketing procedures (e.g., to set agreements among the co-op members on production quotas).

Special-purpose temporary organizations are short lived and have very distinctive functions. One good example, general to agriculture but not limited to lettuce, was the Citizens for a Fair Farm Labor Law created in 1976 to combat Proposition 14, which agricultural growers saw as threatening their interests and strengthening the position of the United Farm Workers Union. In many cases the creation of such organizations is supported by the California Farm Bureau; sometimes these organizations are created for special purposes and then are endowed with permanent existence; in other cases, once the fight is over, the organization is permitted to expire. Another example of such a special-purpose organization, consisting heavily but certainly not exclusively of lettuce growers, is found in the Citizens for Government Fairness. This organization of Imperial Valley growers was formed at the end of 1977 to fight the inclusion of the Imperial Valley in the regulations being considered by the federal government with respect to enforcement of the 160-acre limitation.[15]

The character of a permanent organization demonstrates, at one and the same time, the strengths and weaknesses of such an organization. In summary, we will argue that grower organization is most coherent when dealing with an external force, and in particular, labor; weaker when dealing with external forces that are more powerfully integrated, such as government; and weakest when dealing with internal regulation. These patterns become clearer by examining various forms of grower organization in and around lettuce production.

Grower-shipper associations

The keystone organization of lettuce producers is the Western Growers and Shippers Association. Formed in 1926, its major functions can be seen in its committee structure: four years after formation it had committees on advertising, legislation, and traffic (*Western Grower and Shippers*, January 1930). The function of the advertising committee was to advertise lettuce so as to encourage an increase in its consumption. The legislative committee watched Sacramento and Washington, D.C., observing the specialized problems of growers but also being concerned with other problems such as the flow of Mexican labor. The traffic committee represented the grower-shippers' interests with respect to railways and their facilities.

The grower-shipper associations began after the Western Growers Association, and their origins can be most clearly seen in the labor difficulties the growers confronted in the mid-1930s. The major association, the Grower-Shipper Vegetable Association of Central California (GSVA) was formed in 1930 and incorporated in 1935 (Lamb 1942, p. 92; U.S. Senate 1941, Part 73, 26969–26971). The GSVA had, from its inception, a key integrative function with respect to labor. When packing shed workers struck in Salinas in the spring of 1936, it was the GSVA that organized grower response and was primarily responsible for the defeat of the strike. Labor organization existed prior to this period. Lamb (1942), for example, notes strikes in central California in 1928, and in Imperial in 1930 and again in Salinas in 1933 (Lamb 1942, Chapters 8, 9). The Imperial Valley strikes were so important (see Bernstein 1970, pp. 160–8) that growers organized two associations – the anti-Communist Association and the Imperial Valley Growers and Shippers Protective Association – the latter has been described as a "suborganization" of the Western Growers Association (Lamb 1942, p. 240). About the same time, the California Farm Bureau was organizing the Associated Farmers to combat the burgeoning militancy of farm workers (Chambers 1952; Jamieson 1945). Thus it was the attempts at organizing farm workers that gave rise to the host of grower-shipper associations in Salinas, Imperial, Oxnard, Yuma, Santa Maria, and elsewhere.

The grower-shipper associations showed marked capacity to resist the onslaught of unionization until the early 1970s. Until then, they maintained sufficient strength so that when Bud Antle signed a contract with the Teamsters Union his firm was excluded from the organization. In early summer 1971, when the then United Farm Workers Organizing Committee (UFWOC) successfully signed contracts with table grape growers in the Delano, California area, lettuce growers panicked at the possibility that Chavez would turn his organizing attentions toward them. The grower community, organized through the GSVA in Salinas, decided to sign contracts with the Teamsters Union as a way of excluding Chavez (Friedland and Thomas 1974). It is worth noting that the lettuce growers in doing this acted in disagreement with the California Farm Bureau, which was, at the time, urging growers to take the "third way," signing neither with the Teamsters nor UFWOC but creating their own special-purpose organizations, which would provide social services equivalent to those offered by UFWOC and thereby negating the need for trade unionism.[16]

During the early 1970s GSVA constituted the primary force resisting the entry of the UFWOC (later the United Farm Workers–UFW) into lettuce. This resistance was only partially successful, for the largest firm, Inter Harvest, agreed to sign a contract with the Chavez forces despite the hostilities of the other grower-shippers because of the vulnerability of United Brands to a consumer boycott and the ostensible liberal connections of Eli Black, the head of United (McCann 1976: Chap. 10). More recently the GSVA remains the primary organization that most grower-shippers draw upon for advice in contract negotiations and industrial relations practices. In this respect Sun Harvest and Bud Antle are most removed from GSVA with respect to labor practices, but most of the other grower-shippers coordinate their activities on labor through the organization. Grower-shipper associations in other districts play similar roles, although there are differences in tone among areas. The grower-shipper organization in Santa Maria has been particularly engaged in maintaining relationships with the Teamsters Union; the Imperial Association is generally opposed to all forms of unionism.

Before discussing attempts at other forms of organization that have been less successful, we should note that lettuce producers are affiliated with a variety of other organizations that operate at the national level. Most of the relationships among organizations are informal rather than formal; they are, nevertheless, important. Not only are organizations such as the Western Growers and Shippers Association and the grower-shipper associations linked to the California Farm Bureau, but they are also tied to such organizations as the National Council of Agricultural Employers (NCAE), the organization that oversees national policies and practices with respect to the flow of agricultural labor and its regulation. Lettuce growers are also linked to the United Fresh Fruit and Vegetable Association (UFFVA), an organization that incorporates producers, distributors, and transporters of fresh produce. UFFVA is a more diffuse organization than NCAE because the latter has a special purpose whereas the former is intended to conjoin interest groups. Thus NCAE produces agreements among its constituencies around labor issues although there still exist important differences of opinion based on differential interests.[17]

If growers have been relatively successful in creating organizations with respect to workers and utilizing those organizations as instrumentalities, they have been less successful, though far from unsuccessful, in organizing with respect to other external forces, particularly governments. To demonstrate their successes and failures here we turn to several cases.

The Central California Lettuce Producers Cooperative

This organization was created in 1972 to "serve as a meeting ground for the lettuce producers to come together and agree on pricing policy" (Federal Trade Commission 1977, pp. 39, 52). Prosecuted by the Federal Trade Commission (FTC) for restraining competition, the cooperative members successfully litigated the initial restraint order of an administrative law judge. For several years, during litigation, the cooperative was moribund but was not permitted to perish. Rather, it constituted the organized effort of lettuce growers to litigate with the FTC. In this respect, the capacity of organization was notable vis-à-vis the federal agency. Despite its victory over the FTC, the cooperative has been less successful in performing its purpose of helping to raise the price of lettuce through restraining production of its members. The price of lettuce, in the production season following the legal victory of the growers, remained disastrously low. Thus this case points out that growers were successful in organizing to protect their interests with respect to the FTC but were not able to utilize the co-op to restrict production.

Lettuce promotion

A somewhat similar capacity for organization can be seen in the attempts of lettuce producers to develop an organization for the promotion of lettuce, for example, to advertise lettuce nationally to increase its sale. Typically, the major vehicle for such promotion is the marketing order, a legal means whereby growers of a given commodity can assess themselves for a particular purpose such as promotion. There already exists a marketing order for research in lettuce, which takes the form of the California Iceberg Lettuce Research Program. Lettuce growers sought to avail themselves of their legal rights by voting a marketing order for promotion.

Marketing orders are not created solely through action by any given group of growers; California law requires the approval of the State Director of Agriculture. In 1975, after nine months of inaction dictated by the opposition of Governor Brown to the marketing order, the promotional order was rejected (*Packer* 1975). Lettuce growers promptly turned to another means to accomplish the same purpose: the introduction of a bill in the state legislature that would do exactly the same thing as accomplished through the proposed marketing order. The Western Growers Association threw its support to the bill creating the California Iceberg Lettuce Commission and, as a result, this bill was finally adopted by the legislature. Governor Brown did not veto the bill. This case demonstrates the capacity of growers to organize with respect to government as an external agency.

But if grower-shippers of lettuce have been quite successful in creating organizations to deal with external forces, they have been much less successful in regulating the relationships among themselves with respect to production. Just as labor and its supply constitute a problem for grower-shippers, and one they have been successful in overcoming, grower-shippers also have a major problem with respect to price. A consequence has been that the lettuce grower-shippers have continually sought, although unsuccessfully, to develop an organization to control lettuce prices.

The previously cited case of the Lettuce Producers Cooperative is an example. This case represents the most recent of a great many attempts by lettuce grower-shippers to control price, none of which has been effective. Fundamentally, the problem of price deals with the multiplicity of lettuce growers, on the one hand, compounded by the way in which lettuce grows and the inelasticity of demand, on the other. As noted earlier, despite the existence of a number of large firms in lettuce production, there also exists a multiplicity of smaller firms. In each firm, decisions are made with respect to lettuce production with management personnel making guesses about the condition of weather, the state of the market, and other factors.

Thus, at any given moment, decisions are made with respect to planting that could produce an oversupply of lettuce or a great shortage. These factors are sufficiently uncertain so that a few speculative growers are willing to take a flyer on a small acreage of lettuce in the expectation, or hope, that rain may occur at a given moment in a major production district, thereby impeding the harvest of lettuce and raising the price. With a sizable number of large and medium-sized grower-shippers and an unknown number of small-time speculators, the price of lettuce can be highly variable. At the same time, because of weather and other geophysical circumstances, conditions can be created to produce sharp rises or drops in production. Rain in one portion of a district can seriously delay harvesting and create shortages that produce sharp price increases. Or the end of the season in one district can overlap seriously with the onset of the season in another, thereby producing a lettuce glut.

At the same time, lettuce demonstrates what economists refer to as "inelasticity of demand." Individual consumers of lettuce purchase relatively small amounts weekly and will purchase lettuce in largely the same volume irrespective of price. If the price of lettuce drops, few consumers will increase their consumption; and it is only when the price goes very high that consumers will seek substitutes or cease buying lettuce.

With the combination of such circumstances, lettuce prices are highly variable. One solution to the problem is to cut production on some kind of "prorated" basis in which grower-shippers agree among themselves on some limits, prorated among the different growers according to their share of the market. Prorating, however, has not been very successful because individual growers will violate the prorate agreements, which generally are not legally enforceable, if they see an opportunity to sell lettuce at a higher price than their competitors. Attempts were made in the late 1960s and early 1970s to create a marketing order for southwestern producers but growers could not agree on the order (see U.S. Senate 1975, p. 40). Other similar attempts on a localized basis, including the Central California Cooperative, have not been any more successful, although the organizational basis for such cooperation has been established. Thus organization for price regulation has not yet succeeded with lettuce grower-shippers.

Somewhat similar frustrations can be seen in the successes and failures of the California Iceberg Lettuce Research Program (CILRP). The program became effective in 1973 after application of marketing order procedures of the state of California. CILRP has been successful in funding a variety of projects, including research on breeding, seeds, diseases, and growth rates. Research has also been focused on handling lettuce after shipment, particularly to study the ability of lettuce to be shipped internationally, as well as in bulk containers, a development that could be important to mechanized harvesting practices. Other forms of lettuce handling through "tubing" have also been researched. The main research effort on mechanized harvesting, however, has been conducted through the U.S. Department of Agriculture at its Salinas station and through the University of California, Davis, in its Department of Agricultural Engineering rather than through CILRP. Research into mechanized harvesting was rejected by the Director of Agriculture of the state of California (see CILRP 1976, p. i).

Although grower-shippers have been successful in creating CILRP and getting some research under way, they have been less successful in agreeing on how to utilize this research.[18] Individual growers can take advantage of research on breeding practices or on exports, but growers are unable to reach agreement on standard practices involved in the shipment of lettuce. Thus most receivers complain about the "bulge pack" in lettuce, where lettuce heads are stuffed into cartons so that some bulge develops in the sides (Drossler 1976, p. 46). Yet, only one grower-ship-per, Bud Antle, has moved to a palletization process that helps to elimi-nate the bulge pack, and no grower-shippers have sought to develop bulk containers for shipment because of transport insufficiencies.

This overall assessment demonstrates that grower-shippers of lettuce have strong capacities for organization and for utilizing organizations as weapons but, at the same time, their own self-interest limits what can be accomplished through such organizations. These strengths and limitations will have a bearing on our discussion of the conditions under which har-vest mechanization can occur, which we will discuss in the next chapter.

The state of the art in lettuce research

Because lettuce is a highly organized system of production, which has been functioning since the 1920s, it is a system that has benefited from long and sustained research. Reference has already been made to many of the research developments that produced change in the system. We have not, however, attempted to delineate much of the research involved with varieties, rates of growth under differential weather conditions, and the like, because this type of material is not germane to the analysis at hand. Here we will only examine various forms of research and techno-logical change related to potential mechanization. For these purposes we will look at preharvest, harvest, and postharvest research activities.

Research in preharvest activities

Much of the research involved in preharvest activities is concerned with seed varieties and rates of growth. Most of this work is not related di-rectly to a mechanization transition and would be continued irrespective of the state of mechanization research. Perhaps the only sort of research that *might* be conducted in this form would consist of research aimed at producing a lettuce head that was square. A "square lettuce," in the unlikely event that it were producible, would fit together remarkably well with mechanized harvesting of lettuce, because the technology of wrap-ping is geared toward the utilization of square rather than for round surfaces. Thus lettuce could be mechanically wrapped if the lettuce were placed on a flat tray. This option is unfeasible because it would occupy much greater space than is presently utilized in packing lettuce. Because so much lettuce is transported over thousands of miles, the loss of space would be uneconomical. Were a lettuce variety to be developed that had a flat surface at its base, it might be machine wrappable. This, however, is a somewhat improbable situation.[19]

One present development is being conducted without specific concern for mechanized harvesting. Nevertheless, this development, involving the growth of lettuce seedlings in greenhouses and their transplantation, appears to be compatible with mechanized harvesting. The process, if successful, will probably eliminate the need for much of the preharvest activity involving thinning and weeding, the most labor-intensive activities in the preharvest period of lettuce production. Hence we will provide some detail on the character of this research and development.

The relevant development on seedlings is being conducted by one grower-shipping firm, Bud Antle, Inc.[20] The basic process involves the preparation of lettuce seedlings in greenhouses to a proper state of maturity and their transplantation to the fields in a semimechanized procedure. Typical of organizational structures in lettuce is a distinctive subsidiary, Salinas Transplants Company, which Antle has created to develop the procedures for growing and transplanting seedlings. In many respects lettuce seedlings technology is following the already established techniques developed in celery production where seedlings are often transplanted rather than planting seeds directly in the fields.

In the Antle process, seedlings are grown in fifty-two greenhouses, each of which can handle 3,024 trays or a total of 360,000 plants per greenhouse. These greenhouses "can produce plants for about 25 percent of Bud Antle's California operation" (Razee 1976). Most greenhouse space, however, is dedicated to celery seedlings and the lettuce procedures are still being tried experimentally. If the development operates well, capacity for expansion to 250 greenhouses exists.

The basic process, known as "speedlings" production, was developed by George Todd of Ruskin, Florida. It involves utilizing polystyrene trays, each of which has 120 inverted pyramids formed in the tray. The trays are prepared on a semi-automated basis by being filled with a "growing medium" consisting of peat and vermiculite. After automatic filling, the trays move on conveyors through a series of large brushes that sweep away excess material. A hole is then "dibbled" in each cell and a single seed is mechanically injected. The trays are visually inspected by an operator to ensure that each hole has a seed. Then the trays go through a machine that sprinkles a layer of vermiculite on top to cover the seeds. After being lightly sprayed with water, the trays are moved into the open, palletized, and then moved to the greenhouses.

In the greenhouses, the trays are suspended on rails 30 inches off the floor. The plants are irrigated by a self-propelled water system with booms that extend over the trays. The irrigation water carries fertilizer and, as needed, insecticides and fungicides. The plants emerge in three or four days and by twenty-five to thirty days a rootball has formed. When the rootballs are firm the trays are loaded in plywood bins, each holding 120 trays. A trailer holds thirty bins of about 400,000 plants, enough for about fourteen acres.

The plant trays are loaded on the transplanter, a specially built vehicle that is towed behind a tractor through the fields. Several workers, usually women, sit on this machine, riding backwards. They remove the plants from the cells individually and position them on a moving belt. The plants are inserted in the ground mechanically, four rows at a time. "Eventually they hope to get the plants out of the cells without the use of hand labor. The goal is to plant 25 acres a day with two or three people, and then sit back and wait for the crop to be mechanically harvested" (Razee 1976).

The advantages of the seedling system, according to one of the people responsible for its development, are many:

1. There are improved plant populations because the plants are spaced 10.5 inches apart and are staggered rather than placed directly opposite each other in the rows. This provides a count of 31,360 plants per acre, or 1,306 cartons per acre as potential maximum yield. This compares with high yields of 1,000 cartons per acre at present.
2. Weak plants can be eliminated while still in the greenhouse, therefore producing higher yields.
3. There is better pest control because the plants are in the greenhouse when they are youngest and most vulnerable.
4. There is also better weed control because the field can be herbicided before transplantation.
5. There are savings on irrigation labor and on water because the water necessary for germination in the greenhouse is less than in the fields; irrigation in the greenhouse is mechanical and labor is thereby saved.
6. Fertilizer is saved because it is incorporated into the irrigation water and does not have to be drill injected massively as it is when the lettuce seed is planted in the fields.
7. There is a shorter growing time in the fields because the seedlings have controlled temperature conditions in the greenhouses.

8. There may be greater uniformity of any given lettuce field, which would make for a heavier (and more productive) first cutting of the field.

The seedlings system remains to be proven in lettuce production. If it proves effective, however, the consequences, from the point of view of mechanized harvesting, might include:

1. There will be higher capital intensivity in planting with concomitant reduction in labor. Thinning and weeding may become unnecessary, thereby removing a portion of the externalized labor force. These workers will be replaced by a smaller number of internalized workers, for example, permanent employees involved in greenhouse production of seedlings. The process will also reduce, to an unknown extent, the amount of irrigation requirements.

2. There will be much higher control over production scheduling of the fields through this system. The vagaries of temperature and its effects on germination are considerable. As a result, were a mechanical harvester to be used, it could potentially reduce the number of times the machine would have to pass through the fields.

Although the seedling system may become useful concomitant to mechanized harvesting, it remains as yet unproven. Problems with the root system remain and maturation rates and their varying character are still unresolved.

Research in harvest mechanization

Although a considerable amount of small-scale research and experimentation is continually going on with respect to harvest activities, the major efforts currently underway are concerned with the development of a mechanized system for lettuce harvesting. Historically, interest in mechanized lettuce harvesting began in the early 1960s at the University of Arizona and shortly afterward at the University of California, Davis. As the bracero program came to an end in 1964, the California State Legislature was sufficiently concerned to allocate $150,000 in 1965 to support agricultural mechanization research in the University of California's budget (Kelly 1966, p. ii). During this same period several commercial firms built lettuce harvesters anticipating the development of shortages of harvester workers.

The Department of Agriculture Engineering at the University of California, Davis, began research in lettuce harvest mechanization around this time. Between 1964 and 1966 a series of projects produced the technical capability by which lettuce heads could be selected on the basis of firmness by running a roller over the heads calibrated against a spring that gauged the size and firmness of each head (Harriott and Barnes, 1964; Harriott et al. 1964; Garrett et al. 1966).

The mid-1960s' developments did not fully resolve all the technological difficulties in mechanized lettuce harvesting but tended to focus on the problem of selection because lettuce does not mature homgeneously and selection would constitute a major problem in mechanization. On their part, as was indicated earlier, grower-shippers were resolving their labor problems by converting bracero laborers into green card workers and evolving the present crew structure for harvesting lettuce.

Although the sense of immediacy disappeared, research was continued on the selector problem in two locations in California. At the University of California, Davis, Roger Garrett of the Department of Agriculture Engineering pursued a gamma ray device as the key element of a selector principle. At the USDA's Agricultural Research Service station Salinas, Paul Adrian experimented with an X-ray application. Both approaches utilized the principle of a radiation emission passing through the lettuce heads and being received by a detector. If the lettuce was sufficiently dense, the lettuce was considered mature and a signal was sent to a cutting knife, which cut the head. By 1973 considerable progress had been made in the development of auxiliary processes including the problem of elevating the head to a position on the machine where it could be handled (Lenker et al. 1973; *Western Grower and Shipper* 1973, pp. 5–8; *Agricultural Research* 1974, pp. 8–11). Research was also being conducted in New York State along similar lines (Shepardson et al. 1973).

By 1975 two separate prototype harvesters had been developed by Garrett's group at Davis and Adrian's group in Salinas.

The Davis machine involves the utilization of a gamma-ray emitter positioned opposite a detector. The device is mounted in front of the knife and elevating apparatus. As the machine passes down the row, rays are emitted. If the lettuce is sufficiently dense, a signal is sent to the knife, which cuts the lettuce. At the same time, the signal is forwarded to the elevating mechanism, which consists of a series of "fingers" mounted on a wheel. The fingers close on the lettuce head when the signal is received. The wheel rotates as the mechanism moves down the rows and

the lettuce is then elevated upward in a circle. After appropriate elevation, the fingers release the head, which can then be transported by
conveyors as necessary. The Davis prototype has not been developed into
a full-scale machine, although the Bud Antle Company has been developing a prototype based on the Garrett approach that would harvest four
rows of lettuce at a time.

The Salinas machine uses X-rays to detect the density of the heads and
to trigger the cutting knife. The trimming and elevation principles are
different, however, with a set of rubber-fingered conveyors mounted opposite each other. Each lettuce head is held by the conveyors. If the
radiation source has registered sufficient density, a signal triggers a knife,
which cuts the head at the base. The conveyors then carry the cut head to
another trimming knife although this aspect of trimming was still not
technically satisfactory as of mid-1978. The head is then moved through a
series of conveyors to an elevated position where it can be handled in a
variety of ways: further trimmed by hand, packed into cartons, or
conveyed into bins being pulled behind a trailer alongside the harvester.
The machine is much further developed than the Davis machine and was
field tested in August 1977 (Manning 1977). The capacity of the Salinas
machine was reported to be 9,600 heads, or 400 cartons per hour. The
prototype, however, was developed with a capacity to harvest only one
row of lettuce at a time; capacity to cut two rows is easily addable, which
could increase the capability of the machine to 700 cartons per hour. In
theory, this machine could also harvest four rows of lettuce. A potential
problem with both machines always exists with respect to weight. As size
and weight increase, problems with soil compaction increase. Also, the
weight of the machine is a problem under conditions of wet fields when
compaction increases and the machine can become mired.

Thus at present there exist two prototype machines that can potentially
be developed for mechanized harvesting of lettuce fairly quickly, if need
be.[21]

Postharvesting handling

Several major postharvest problems exist and must be resolved before a
transition to mechanization can take place. The capacity of the prototypes
to cut lettuce is, in a sense, greater than the capacity for the lettuce to be
handled after cutting.[22,23] Although machines can be built large enough to
handle the theoretical cutting capacity, their weight would pose problems.

Accordingly, one phase of research has involved the handling of lettuce in bulk containers separated from the machine, whereas another phase of research has been involved with the wrapping of lettuce heads.

Bulk handling represents an application similar to that found in the harvest of processing tomatoes. In this method the lettuce heads are conveyed from the harvesting machine into bulk bins, which are carried on a trailer pulled by a small tractor alongside the harvest machine. Several possible means for handling the lettuce from the trailers are under experimentation. One involves moving the bins to packing facilities either on the edge of the field or at some central packing shed. In this configuration the lettuce heads are moved from the bins by some conveying process to packers who pack them into cartons. The cartons are then treated in the same manner as existing cartons of lettuce.

This process is unsatisfactory to grower-shippers because of insufficient reduction in costs to make the investment in the machine worthwhile. Experiments are, therefore, taking place with the handling of lettuce in bulk containers. Made out of heavy cardboard, these large boxes are intended to carry approximately 250 heads of lettuce. They are carried alongside the machine on a trailer. Once the boxes are full, the trailer is replaced by another trailer with empty boxes. The loaded boxes are moved to a station from which the boxes are placed on a vibrating device, which shakes the entire assemblage briefly and compacts the lettuce. The box is then sealed and moved to the coolers. From this point the box is handled in the same manner as the lettuce cartons except for its size and weight, which require its movement by conveyor and/or forklift throughout the entire distribution chain until the lettuce reaches the retailer. This fact, in itself, poses problems because the utilization of the large box would have ramifications throughout the entire distribution system.

Lettuce wrapping by machine represents the second major problem in postharvest handling. At present no satisfactory wrapping technology exists that could produce a mechanically wrapped lettuce head equivalent to that produced by hand. Experimentation was undertaken until 1978 with techniques to film wrap the lettuce mechanically. One concept, developed by Garrett at Davis, involved wrapping lettuce in "tubes" of five with serrations between each head. Each tube would be inserted in a box that would carry a total of 250 heads stacked five deep. Other concepts involving individual heads being wrapped are also being explored. At this writing, most of these wrapping experiments have stopped.

The resolution of the wrapping technology could produce a major shift toward harvest mechanization, an argument that will be examined in greater detail in the next chapter.

Carton palletization represents an additional area of experimentation conducted by Antle up to 1978. This process involves the packing of lettuce cartons into pallets and constructing them into cubes capable of being handled by forklift from the field to the wholesale distributor.

The process involves loading cartons on to pallets carried on trucks, which ride through the fields after the lettuce is packed into cartons (Bricker 1976). The cartons are layered, glue is placed on top of each layer, and additional layers are added to a total of eight. The corners of the cube are supported by wooden rods. The entire cube is then strapped. As each cube is completed by the loaders in the field, they move on to the next. When the truck is loaded, it moves to the vacuum coolers. Here the cubes are forklifted on to conveyors, cooled, moved again by forklift into the trailers. The fit is so tight that the loads must be "shoehorned" into the vehicles. Arriving at distribution terminals, the cubes are forklifted out of the trailers into the cooling rooms where the cubes are broken down into individual cartons for shipment.

This process was developed by Antle to eliminate present damage to lettuce heads, on the one hand, and to deal with a bottleneck in loading the trailers by hand, on the other. This process is potentially adaptable to machine harvesting but it retains the carton package, which would appear to be unsatisfactory to machine harvesting because of the numbers of packers required to be carried on the machine and the resultant problem of weight.

An examination of scientific and technological developments in lettuce production demonstrates that a variety of approaches have been undertaken by public agencies and private companies, each of which could have potential for fitting with mechanized harvesting of lettuce. With the basic technological developments resolved, but with many technical details still unsettled, the potentiality of mechanization of the harvest, and of other segments of the production system, "stands in the wings" ready for adoption. In the next chapter we will consider the conditions under which such a transition can occur.

4. Projected consequences of technological change in the lettuce industry

At any given moment in time, in any production system, a variety of scientific and technological developments may await potential adoption. Although enormous literature on adoption and diffusion practices has developed (Rogers 1962), the adoption of lettuce harvest mechanization poses issues very different from those found in standard literature. Research on this subject focuses on contexts in which there are a great many potential adopters. The problem for researchers, under these circumstances, is to comprehend the conditions under which some people adopt while others delay.

In the present study, the number of potential adopters is exceedingly small, especially when compared to the numbers involved in other production systems. Further, the number of potential machines involved is also very small. Finally, the community of adopters in lettuce production is homogeneous, maintains very close contact and communications, and, indeed, conducts almost continuous discussion and debate on a large number of subjects affecting their system. Under the circumstances the conditions affecting adoption are considerably different from those found in other situations. In assessing the conditions under which mechanized harvesting will begin, we draw considerably from our understanding of the character of the lettuce production system.

This chapter begins with an examination of the conditions under which mechanization of the harvest will occur. In the second section we set out the assumptions that underlie the analysis of the consequences of such a transition. The final section considers the consequences that we anticipate will derive from a shift to mechanized harvesting. This section begins by considering the effects on grower organization. Because we anticipate that the social consequences of mechanized harvesting will be experienced more intensively by the workers involved, we examine the anticipated labor displacement, the changing structure of the labor force, and the reorganization of the work process in greater detail. The analysis of consequences concludes with consideration of the effects on surrounding communities. By projecting significant displacement of workers and stabilization of those workers retained in the industry, we look initially on the effects of mechanization on housing, education, and other social services. The chapter concludes with an examination of projected effects on the Imperial Valley and the adjoining Baja California area.

The conditions for transition to mechanized harvesting

Given the state of the art technologically – that is, the present capacity to make a transition to mechanized harvesting – the most immediate question is: Why do grower-shippers not make the transition? The machine prototype is sufficiently well developed to permit such a transition. Clearly, although further technological refinement is and will be necessary, and although auxiliary aspects of handling and wrapping remain unresolved, the failure of grower-shippers to adopt the new technology cannot be accidental.

This point is further amplified by the experience with harvest mechanization at the end of the *bracero* program in 1964. At that time there was the expectation of a greatly diminished labor supply. Grower-shippers hedged their bets by supporting research to develop a prototype harvester. A technological solution was found but grower-shippers also discovered the feasibility of maintaining the labor supply. Thus they made a deliberate decision to focus on labor rather than to proceed to capital substitution.

Experience of the past decade demonstrates that grower-shippers have preferred a highly labor-intensive system even though the wages earned by the workers involved, in ground-packed lettuce, are very high – probably the highest earned by harvest workers, when they are employed, anywhere in the United States. Although producing high wages for lettuce harvesters, this system is still the lowest cost harvest method available to growers. Since 1971 when unionization of harvest workers began, labor costs have increased with the extension of contractual fringe benefits and the inclusion of farm workers under social security legislation. Despite these increases, labor still constitutes only a small segment of the total cost of production, although small labor savings per head can translate into significant dollar totals given the large number of lettuce heads that are harvested. Cargill and Garrett, for example, place harvest and packing costs of a 39-cent head of lettuce at 2.1 cents or 5.4 percent of the retail price. This compares with 7.1 cents or 18.2 percent, which represent the costs of transportation of the lettuce from west to east.[1] Table 4.1

Table 4.1. *Factor Costs of Lettuce Production and Distribution*

Cost factor	Unit cost Cent/head	Percentage of total	Accumulated Cost Cent/head	Percent of retail
Grow crop to maturity	4.0	10.3	4.0	10.3
Select, harvest, pack	2.1	5.4	6.1	15.6
Standard carton (24 heads)	1.5	3.8	7.6	19.5
Transport-field to cooling station	1.3	3.3	8.9	22.8
Handle, cool, load into transport mode at cooling station	1.3	3.3	10.2	26.2
FOB Salinas price (includes grading, inspection, brokerage fees, grower/shipper profits)	2.3	5.9	12.5	32.0
Transport to eastern distribution center	7.1	18.2	19.6	50.3
Handle at distribution center	1.4	3.6	21.0	53.8
Retail store cost upon arrival (includes storage, handling, overhead, wholesaler profits, etc.)	5.0	12.8	26.0	66.7
Remove lettuce from cooler, trim, wrap and display	4.4	11.3	30.4	77.9
Retail price to consumer (includes storage, merchandising overhead, retailer profits, etc.)	8.6	22.0	39.0	100.0

Source: Cargill and Garrett 1975, p.8.

shows the various cost inputs for a 39-cent lettuce head in a retail store in the east (Cargill and Garrett 1975).

With a labor-intensive process that is extremely efficient, however, grower-shippers are reluctant to experiment with a new harvest system that remains uncertain, with problems of wrapping and handling still unresolved and whose prospects remain cloudy. The conditions for a transition to mechanized harvesting apparently have not yet arrived. We, therefore, turn to a consideration of the conditions that may induce mechanization:

1. Some form of blockage in the supply of labor and/or its control.
2. The development of conditions in which sharply increased labor savings can be obtained through mechanization.
3. The possibility that a sharp increase may occur in the costs of transportation that might affect the harvest labor supply.

Blockages to labor supply or labor control

The potential forms of blockages of the supply of labor are many, although most are unlikely; the forms of constraints on control over the labor force, in contrast, are fewer but quite possible.

Three fundamental impediments could occur in the supply of harvest workers. First, governmental actions by either the U.S. or Mexican governments could impede, delay, or hinder the supply of labor. The overwhelming number of harvesters that ground pack lettuce are Mexican nationals. Recent work (Thomas 1980c) suggests that many of them maintain residences in Baja California. From Mexico, they *commute* across the border on a daily basis during the winter season and *migrate* for longer periods when lettuce is being produced beyond commuting distance. Any action taken by either government that would obstruct movement across the border would confront employers with labor supply problems. Grower-shippers, however, worry little about these prospects and with good reason. There is slight likelihood, for example, that the Mexican government will take action to interfere with border crossing. Mexico has an ongoing serious problem of unemployment internally, and also its lettuce harvesters provide income for several thousand families living in Mexico. Although a breakdown in Mexican – U.S. relations could possibly lead to a blockage of movement across the border, such a breakdown is not politically envisionable at the moment. From the U.S. viewpoint, it is clear from action, if not from policy statements, that there is no real desire to slow or stop the movement of Mexican workers into the United States. Despite continual flurries of publicity about illegal border crossings and much discussion about the numbers of *sindocumentos* (undocumented workers) in the United States, continued movement across the border indicates that de facto United States policy is *not* to hinder mobility. Indeed, there is reason to believe that the Immigration and Naturalization Service (INS) and the Border Patrol look upon the movement of illegals with less of a jaundiced eye than policy statements indicate. Thus, although governmental impediments to mobility could affect the labor supply, this prospect appears unlikely.

A second form of blockage could conceivably occur through the organization of workers in Mexico through the agricultural affiliate of the Confederation of Mexican Workers (CTM). Such unionization might impede labor supply, particularly if it were to improve wages significantly and to make the prospects for agricultural employment in Mexico more attractive. This prospect is also remote. The CTM has not been overly concerned with the conditions of agricultural workers in Mexico and, even if it were to do so, the probabilities that Mexican wage rates could become competitive with California's rates, are minuscule. CTM has shown little or no interest in border-crossing workers, in any case, and the Mexican unions, like their government sponsor, are probably happy that some workers are working in the United States, thereby relieving internal unemployment pressures.

A third impediment of supply might occur through a breakdown in the process by which replacement workers are recruited. There is some evidence that crew members come from geographically proximate areas in Mexico (e.g., "the same village") and that individual crew members maintain contacts in the villages through which new members are recruited. Any policies impeding interaction with the villages, assuming the evidence to be accurate, would impede the self-reproduction process of the crews. If, for example, the U.S. government made border crossing extremely cumbersome, as occurred for a short period during a drive against drug trafficking, the greencard lettuce harvesters might find it necessary to move to the United States, thereby possibly reducing contacts with home villages. Crew members might begin to recruit replacements from potential pools within the United States because lettuce harvesting is, comparatively speaking, well-paid employment. But this eventuality is also unlikely, for the probability of movement blockage is remote.

If the prospects for impediments in supply are small, the possibilities of blockages in control, from the viewpoint of grower-shippers, are much greater.

At present, grower-shippers effectively have control over conditions of employment of lettuce workers: As employers, they set the standards as to what gets harvested and packed and the methods of conducting work. Grower-shippers have less control over payment to harvesters because the group piece-work system is significantly controlled by the crews. Grower-shippers, for example, have been notably hesitant to attempt to cut wage rates of naked-lettuce harvesters, despite their very high earnings.

One potential anomaly may develop with union organization. Historically, in most employer–union contracts, employers have the right to change piece rates whenever a "change in method" is made. This fact has been utilized to cut piece rates whenever they get too high, from the employer's point of view. Lettuce harvesters have resisted such tendencies in the past because of the importance of the self-reproducing crew system. With unionism, however, and the changing character of the crew, lettuce employers may begin to resemble employers elsewhere more closely; thus one benefit of union organization, for employers, may be to create the conditions under which piece rates can be cut.

A more likely prospect, however, is that unionization of harvesters will significantly impede the levels of control that employers have come to expect (Thomas 1980c). Lettuce growers, as noted in Chapter 3, have been somewhat less than enthusiastic about unionism. Although grower-shippers now are prepared to live with unions such as the United Farm Workers (UFW), doubtless they have little enthusiasm for it; equally, there can be little uncertainty that, almost universally, employers will seek to limit the effects of unionism on their organizational control (Razee 1981).

If the United Farm Workers Union continues to conduct itself more as a "social movement" than a union, to use the formulations of agricultural employers, union–management relations will be troublesome. It is in these circumstances that concern for control by employers becomes maximal. Even with contracts, the blockage of control by a union that defines its mandate broadly can be difficult. Employers might find, for example, that they cannot order workers into a field that has been recently sprayed with pesticides. This is an issue that has raised considerable, and legitimate, passion in the recent past since the UFW has been in disagreement with many employers as to how quickly a field can be entered after chemical application. Disagreements are also endemic over second and third harvests because income becomes problematic after the first harvest of a field. With a grievance apparatus common to collective agreements, harvesters may become less pliant to employer pressures on these matters. Similar difficulties may arise over the no-strike provisions normal in most collective agreements. Typical of such clauses is the one found in the agreement between the UFW and Inter-Harvest:

A. There shall be no strikes, slowdowns, boycotts, interruptions of work by the union nor shall there by any lockout by the Company . . .
C. Workers covered by this agreement shall not engage in any strike, slowdown or other interruption of work, which action is not approved by the union.[2]

Although this is standard contractual language, its existence does not always convince workers that they should not stop work when a grievance arises. At the moment, grower-shippers, still learning to live with the reality of unionism, have short tempers, and a rash of wildcat strikes might make the prospect of mechanized harvesting more attractive. As was noted when electronic sorting of tomatoes was developed, "Machines don't strike."

Even more important than these considerations, which are often a function of early unionism, is what happens over the long run in union–management relations. Managements realize that bottlenecks exist in production about which little can be done without changing work organization. One such example is in the case of the Antle Company and its move to palletization in the fields, discussed in the previous chapter. Because loading was controlled by a small number of workers who constituted a bottleneck in production, management reorganized production to load the cartons directly onto pallets in the fields. Although the firm announced its satisfaction that no workers lost their jobs through this process, the fact remains that the change in the work process eliminated the bottleneck, or, more accurately, the group of workers that effectively controlled the bottleneck.

A potential example of how mechanization might fit in with the bottleneck effect can be found in the case of harvesting winter lettuce in southern California and Arizona. Workers reporting for work in the Inter-Harvest contract are guaranteed four hours of pay. If workers report at 8:00 a.m., in winter conditions often work cannot begin until the frost has melted. Lettuce cannot be harvested until it is free of frost because handling before melting initiates decay. Workers must wait, therefore, unpaid, before they can work the four hours guaranteed them under the contract. It is hardly surprising if workers find such a situation less than attractive. Thus workers might impede the harvest by refusing to work unless they are paid waiting time; or more probably, the union may seek to include waiting time into the contract, thereby raising the employer's labor costs.

The potential impediments to labor control provide some indication of the conditions under which employers might find the transition to mechanized harvesting more attractive than at present. One additional possibility should also be kept in mind in terms of the issue of control – the existence of the harvest machine represents a factor to be taken into consideration by growers and unions in their relations with each other. Collective bargaining processes, in other words, could be affected as much by the potential adoption of the harvest machine as by its actuality.

How growers and unions will adapt to such a situation is difficult to estimate because the relationships between employers and the union representing field-workers, the United Farm Workers Union, are not yet fully institutionalized. The threat of mechanization has been used as a bargaining tool by managements in other industries, however, and the possible application of this approach in lettuce production cannot be ignored.

Production cost reductions through mechanization

A major reason that grower-shippers manifest little interest in making the transition to mechanized harvesting is that they see little indication of significant savings to be obtained at the moment. Transition entails the shift from a tested and tried system to one with considerable uncertainties. If the uncertainties with respect to supply or control of the labor force increase, grower-shippers will probably be prepared to accept the uncertainties of a new technology. Until then, however, or until the savings potential through the new technology becomes clearer, the reluctance of grower-shippers to shift is understandable.

What, then, are the short-range prospects for effecting savings in production costs with the harvesting machine? We have already indicated one: the condition in which there were to be a sharp increase in the demand for winter lettuce and therefore in its price without expanding production areas. Under such circumstances, grower-shippers would have to create the conditions in which more lettuce could be harvested under the restricted daylight and temperature conditions of winter harvesting. To increase crew sizes would constitute one potential solution; the other would be to utilize the machine as an adjunct to existing crews.

Grower-shippers would probably move toward the latter solution with considerable hesitation. This kind of change would involve sizable investments not only in the capital equipment represented by the machine but also in the complex of procedures necessary to implement a new system of work organization. The investment in the machine alone (estimated at over $100,000 each) would be discouraging; but the implementation of a new work organization paralleling the existing production system would also raise serious doubts for most employers. To make such a high investment and to maintain the machine for part-time utilization is somewhat unlikely. It is not, however, inconceivable; in the event of such a sustained surge of winter lettuce to $10 a carton or higher, grower-shippers with strong capital capacity could move to mechanized harvesting to serve as an adjunct to the existing system. This eventuality is not only unlikely but, in addition, were it to occur, it would constitute a slow and only partial transition to mechanized harvesting.

A more likely condition yielding substantial savings could be obtained if mechanized harvesting contributed to cost reductions *after* the harvest, that is, in handling and distribution. The present capacity of the machine to cut and trim lettuce exceeds the capacity to handle and pack it. This proved to be the situation at the time of the transition to mechanized tomato harvesting. When that transition occurred, the original process for handling the tomatoes, packing into lugs (wooden boxes) containing 50 pounds of fruit, was initially maintained. It was quickly discovered that the lugs could not handle the volume of fruit produced by the machine. Adaptations were successively made, which culminated in an automated system that delivered the fruit to over-the-road gondolas, which could be hauled from the fields to the processing plants.

Mechanized lettuce harvesting presents a similar problem. The August 1977 prototype tests demonstrated that, although a single row cutter was slower than a crew of workers, the machine potentially can cut more than a crew. The human crew, however, cuts its lettuce into cartons, whereas the machine presently can only handle lettuce in bulk. There is not only considerable resistance by receivers to accepting lettuce in bulk but also other potential impediments exist to handling the lettuce in this manner. Until this resistance is dissolved *or* a variant system of handling is developed, the prospects for mechanized harvesting are not strong.

This, then, directs attention of the technologists to the problems of packing and handling the lettuce. One such technology was explored at the University of California, Davis, until recently (Cargill and Garrett 1975). This involved the wrapping of lettuce in "tubes" of five. The plastic wrapper film between each head was serrated to permit detachment of individual heads by consumers after display. Tubes of five were inserted in a large cardboard container holding 250 heads. Cartons could be forklifted; they would also be collapsible and returnable.

If such a system were adopted, it would permit the integration of machine harvesting and trimming of the lettuce with machine wrapping and handling so that the need for direct human labor would be substantially reduced. The number of heads, 250, "is suitable for a large number of retail supermarkets" (Cargill and Garrett 1975, p.9). The developers of this approach also argue that a trailer could carry 19,500 heads instead of the present conventional load of 18,240, thus increasing transportation capacity by 6.9 percent – a significant savings when transportation constitutes such a considerable proportion of total costs.

"Tube and cube" technology, as it has been named, might introduce significant savings in lettuce production and distribution costs although the increased capital costs to implement the process are still unknown:

1. It would reduce the number of workers involved in the wrapping and packing of lettuce substantially. Indeed, it potentially could reduce the thirty-six-person crew of ground pack harvesters, and thirty-three-person crew of wrap pack harvesters to a crew of six to ten workers: a driver, two inspector-trimmers, two workers monitoring the insertion of the tubes in the cartons, one forklift driver, and several auxiliary workers necessary until a smooth-running production process has been developed.
2. It could produce source-wrapped lettuce as a "normal" feature of lettuce production instead of being something for which receivers must pay an extra $1.25 per carton. This system could make wrapped lettuce competitive with naked lettuce and wrapped lettuce probably could be produced at costs approximating those of ground packing.
3. It would improve the economies of transportation by almost 7 percent.

In sum, the development of a wrapping and handling technology as an adjunct of mechanized harvesting could create the conditions for substantial savings. Assuming acceptance by handlers, retailers, and consumers, the conditions would be created for a rapid transition to mechanized harvesting. This transition, it should be emphasized, is being projected only after the technology of wrapping and handling becomes resolved as a mechanized process.

A variant condition would be one in which the demand for source-wrapped lettuce increases dramatically. At present, wrapped lettuce constitutes about 20 percent of production, but the importance of source-wrapped lettuce is continually increasing. The advantages of wrapping high quality lettuce in the fields were explained in the previous chapter. If there are dramatic increases in demand, interest of grower-shippers in mechanized harvesting will increase even before a new wrapping and handling technology is developed, because mechanically harvested lettuce can probably be wrapped more efficiently and at greater cost savings on assembly lines rather than as at present, where the lettuce is wrapped on mobile conveyors. If these conditions occurred, grower-shippers might turn to bulk handling of lettuce from the machine to packing sheds, the system that prevailed until the 1950s, or to wrapping and packing the lettuce in portable sheds moved close to the lettuce fields.

The prospects for increasing demand for source-wrapped lettuce are very good but it is unlikely that there will be a dramatic increase. Accordingly, we do not believe that this particular condition for mechanized transition is significant.

Increases in transportation costs

One additional set of circumstances, more likely to occur, could create the basis for mechanization, that is, continuous sharp increases in the costs of transportation could lead to a shift of lettuce production from California and Arizona eastward, possibly to the eastern seaboard. This in turn might require mechanized harvesting because of the shortage of experienced harvesters in the East.

Transportation constitutes the single largest factor in lettuce production and distribution in midwestern and eastern markets. Table 4.1 showed the importance of transportation costs; there is little prospect for these costs to drop. A shift back to rail transportation could reduce transportation costs, but American railways are apparently unable to maintain competitive delivery schedules with trucks. Although some grower-shippers would prefer to return to rail shipments, it is unlikely that five-day delivery by rail will become possible in the foreseeable future. This means that lettuce distribution remains linked to truck transport and to dependence on petroleum for fuel. With the continuing increases in the cost of petroleum, western lettuce growers may have to consider moving production sources closer to the consumption areas (Leeper 1980).

One factor that could impede movement would be land ownership. Grower-shippers geared to land leasing rather than to ownership have less of a vested interest in remaining in western production than those who own land. Increased costs of transportation could make Florida lettuce much more competitive with western lettuce. Florida production remains only a negligible portion of U.S. production, constituting only 1.75 percent (by weight) in 1979. Although technical problems have impeded Florida's expansion into lettuce production, research is moving forward to develop new lettuce varieties suited to Florida's soils and climate (Waterfield, 1976).

Increased transportation costs would increase costs to consumers or reduce profit margins to grower-shippers. Although the demand for lettuce is relatively inelastic, sharp increases in the price of lettuce could reduce the demand for western lettuce and make Florida lettuce more attractive. Some western growers, under these circumstances, might consider transferring production operations to the eastern seaboard. This would entail major adaptations in the production system. However, as has been shown, lettuce is a production system built on mobility between different loci dependent on geophysical conditions. The adaptation to a different set of conditions along the eastern seaboard would inevitably create many complications but could become more attractive if transportations costs continue to increase.

A shift of production to the East inevitably raises the prospect for a transition to mechanized harvesting. Present harvest workers are accustomed to the western loop in which they move around California and Arizona. Many workers still maintain a firm foothold in Mexico for kinship, economic, and cultural reasons. With a shift of production eastward, present harvesters would have to move into very different circumstances, possibly basing themselves in Florida and moving with a new loop. In any case it would become impossible to retain the kinds of attachments that presently exist with a Mexican base. Although some workers might be prepared to make such a transition, others would not.

On their part, were western grower-shippers to establish an eastern system of production they would undoubtedly seek to establish a production process that would not inherit intact the organization of production presently found in California and Arizona. Even if they were reluctant to shift to machine harvesting, grower-shippers would seek to undermine the autonomy and independence of western harvest crews. The development of alternative crews based on utilization of an eastern labor supply, composed of Black domestic workers, Puerto Ricans, and Mexican workers who have settled in Florida, is also conceivable. But the problem of labor supply would increase the interest of grower-shippers in mechanized harvesting, and many might seek a "permanent" solution to their labor problems by shifting to machine harvest.

Assumptions about the transition to mechanized harvesting

Before proceeding to our specification of the social consequences of mechanized lettuce harvesting, we must set out the assumptions underlying the projections. As noted earlier, social projection is a hazardous enterprise; at a minimum it requires a clear set of specifications. We will attempt to set out these assumptions explicitly so that readers can critically assess them prior to examining the projections:

1. No transition to mechanized harvesting is likely until the packing and handling problems are resolved, particularly with respect to the wrapping of lettuce.
2. The number of workers involved in lettuce harvesting is somewhere between 6,000 and 7,500. Of these, we estimate that 60 percent work at ground packing and the other 40 percent are involved in wrap packing. The numbers of workers involved in harvesting lettuce for shredding is sufficiently small so that we can ignore them.
3. Once the technologies of packing and handling are resolved, we assume that the rate of adoption of mechanized harvesting will be extremely rapid, that is, it will occur as fast as the machines can be built, probably in about three years.

The bases for these assumptions have been previously specified in Chapter 3; here we are only stating explicitly that the social projections will be made on the basis of previous analysis.

The issue of the rate of adoption has not yet been discussed and we must clarify the basis for the assumption. The main argument with respect to adoption has been set out by Johnson and Zahara: "Since the machine has not been introduced, there is little basis for estimating the rate of adoption. The experience of mechanization in other crops provided insight on technology adoption, but there is no clear-cut guideline for projection." They thereupon assume a low rate of adoption: "Mechanization is assumed to start in 1980 at a rate of 5 percent rising to 25 percent in 1985" (Johnson and Zahara 1976b, p.379).

Although there is a basis for Johnson and Zahara assuming a low rate of adoption, given the experience in other agricultural situations, we contend that this assumption is incorrect for lettuce. This counterargument is based not only on experience in other commodities but, more particularly, on the specific characteristics of lettuce production.

Experience in other commodities, in particular with processing tomatoes, demonstrates that a very rapid rate of adoption is possible. Tomatoes moved from practically no mechanization to 100 percent in approximately eight years. The rate of adoption of mechanized tomato harvesting is shown in Table 4.2.

Table 4.2. *Rate of Adoption, Mechanical Tomato Harvester, California*

Year	Number of Machines	Percentage of crop Machine harvested
1962	NA	1.0
1963	66	1.5
1964	NA	3:8
1965	224	24.7
1966	736	65.8
1967	1065	81.8
1968	1461	95.1
1969	1510	99.5
1970	1521	99.9

Source: Friedland and Barton 1975, p.27.

A fundamental problem that arises in assessing the assumptions of Johnson and Zahara is that most adoption studies occur in commodities in which there are a sizable volume of producers. Even in the case of tomatoes, the total number of tomato growers in California approximated 4,000, a fairly large number, and this crop experienced a very rapid transition to mechanization.

In the lettuce situation the number of grower-shippers, as already noted, is comparatively small. Table 3.3 shows that forty-seven firms handle 90 percent of California lettuce. From these data we justifiably conclude that the number of decision makers involved in a mechanization transition is very small. We can reasonably assume that firms shipping over 1,000 carlots of lettuce annually can afford the requisite technology when it becomes available; indeed, we might logically believe that most grower-shippers producing 500 carlots of lettuce annually could afford mechanization technology.

Another way to assess the probabilities of adoption is to consider the potential capacity of the harvester. The working prototype harvester developed by the USDA team had an estimated harvest capacity of 450–700 cartons per hour. If a machine were to be operational 300 days per year (6 days a week, 50 weeks of the year) and ten hours each day with a capacity of 600 cartons/hour, it would have an annual harvest capacity of 1,800 carlots.[3] Twelve firms handle this volume of lettuce or more. Thus any decision to adopt at the potential capacity of the harvesting machine could be limited to only twelve firms, which handle over half of California lettuce. On the basis of this analysis we believe the rate of adoption will be much higher than in other commodity situations.

A further factor indicating a rapid rate of adoption can be seen in the history of lettuce production. Lettuce grower-shippers have historically been imitative of new technological developments. When vacuum cooling was introduced, for example, it was quickly adopted in the industry (Smith 1961, Chapter 5; Glass 1966, pp.33–34). Similarly, when film wrap was pioneered by one firm in 1959–60, "By the 1961–62 season as many as ten shippers . . . were using some form of prepackaging" (Padfield and Martin 1965, p.50). If one firm were to demonstrate success with mechanized harvesting, it could be expected that the twelve largest firms would make the transition rapidly.

One factor influencing the rate of adoption will be the speed at which the machines can be built. The number of machines that have to be constructed for a *total* transition to mechanization is very small, perhaps as few as 50 or as many as 150. This number of machines can be built within a period as brief as three years.

The rate of adoption will have significant effects on workers because half or more of the labor force is employed by the twelve largest producers. One expectation, therefore, is that approximately half of the labor force will be affected within a three-year period of the beginning of the transition.

Although our estimates assume a rapid rate of adoption, a note of caution is necessary. Adoption studies are numerous in character (Rogers 1962); however, many of them have focused on adoption practices in more diffused production systems. Relatively little is known, in comparison, about adoption practices in more concentrated systems. Although our expectations are for a rapid adoption rate and transition, it is conceivable that adoption may be very slow for a period of time while grower-shippers experiment with the new harvesting technology.

The social consequences of mechanized lettuce harvesting

Changes in the social system involving the production of lettuce can be projected in three major areas: (1) the organization of the grower-shippers; (2) the numbers and characteristics of workers and the organization of the labor process; (3) and environmentally, the communities where workers and their families live.

Consequences for grower-shippers: concentration

The lettuce production system, as previously noted, is already highly concentrated; a small number of firms produce the bulk of U.S. lettuce. The issue of the domination of production by a small number of producers has been the subject of scholarly analysis and administrative action on the part of federal agencies.[4]

Despite the high degree of concentration, two factors lead to a projection that mechanized harvesting will produce further concentration: (1) There are still many firms shipping 250 carlots or less of lettuce annually. These firms represent that segment of production that will be most severely impacted by mechanization, because (2) The shipment of wrapped lettuce is more heavily concentrated among the larger grower-shippers than the smaller firms. The larger firms, not the smaller grower-shippers, will be able to afford the heavy capital costs of harvesting equipment.

With wrapped lettuce having a competitive edge against naked lettuce as long as quality of product is maintained, it can be anticipated that mechanization will accelerate the trend toward wrapping. Shippers of wrapped lettuce may be able to produce it more competitively vis-à-vis naked lettuce and to make it more attractive to retailers. Some smaller grower-shippers will have the capital capacity to purchase equipment and make the transition to mechanized harvest and wrapping. The development of another cooperative of smaller grower-shippers, or the expansion of the existing co-ops in the Salinas Valley, could facilitate the process of transition for some of the smaller firms. The integration of scheduling required by such machines may change, however, the fundamental character of these growing organizations.

Our projection, therefore, is that there will be increasing concentration in production as a number of the smaller grower-shippers become unable to compete with wrapped lettuce and to make the transition to mechanization because of capital costs. Such grower-shippers may shift to production of other vegetables and/or other agricultural commodities.

The process of concentration with increased capital requirements has been a constant phenomenon in American agriculture; it will be nowhere near as profound and significant as elsewhere because the lettuce production is already concentrated, but there will be additional concentrating effects that will be experienced by smaller grower-shippers.

Concentration of grower-shipper firms, as well as the possibility that these firms will become increasingly attractive to larger multinational corporate entities for takeover purposes, suggests a secondary potential effect – the increased rationalization of the internal organization of the grower-shipper firms. Although little is known publicly about their internal organization, the fact that most firms have developed from family-based entities to larger-scale corporations and that the old mythos of lettuce as a "gambler's crop" still has some residual aspects, indicates that many old, "homegrown," managerial practices may exist within many firms. Concentration of organization, increased capitalization, integration into larger corporate entities, and similar developments indicate that there will be strong tendencies to internally rationalize managerial, administrative, supervisorial, and sales procedures. Grower-shipper firms can, therefore, be expected to experience a variety of internal changes once mechanized harvesting gets under way.

Consequences for workers: labor displacement

Two issues arise with respect to the social effects of technological investment in that component most directly related to the effects on workers and the labor process. First is the question of the number of workers affected, particularly through displacement. Second is the more general issue of the long-range effects of technological change. We will turn initially to some projections about the immediate effects of harvest mechanization on labor displacement and then briefly examine the more general issue.

Table 4.3 summarizes the projections of labor displacement formulated by Johnson and Zahara (1976b) as well as four potential outcomes we have formulated based on varying assumptions. Johnson and Zahara project a 7.8 percent rate of displacement, which is significantly lower than the first of our projections in which we estimate a 43.8 percent displacement rate.

Our first projection is based on an assumption of current machine capacity of 450 cartons per hour with six workers required to operate the machine. It further assumes that only the larger growers, those producing 50 percent of the production, will mechanize. The projected rate of displacement of 43.8 percent is for the entire harvest labor force and data are provided on the basis of this force being 6,000 workers. The second projection provides exactly the same data except that it is based on a different staffing of the machine, assuming the need for twelve workers, at least on an interim basis. This yields a displacement rate of 37.6 percent. The third projection is based on identical conditions as the previous two except that it assumes that all growers producing 500 or more carlots

Table 4.3. *Estimates of Numbers and Rates of Displacement*

Labor displacement		Condition			
	Johnson–Zahara	1	2	3	4
Numbers of workers displaced	360	2628	2256	5073	5220
Rate of displacement (percentage)	7.8	43.8	37.6	83.0	88.9

Condition 1: Assumes 6000 workers, machine capacity of 450 cartons/hour, 50 percent adoption rate for the industry or adoption by the twelve largest grower-shippers.
Condition 2: Same assumptions as Condition 1 but assumes twelve workers required to staff the machines.
Condition 3: Assumes adoption rate of 90 percent or by all grower-shippers producing 500 or more carlots annually.
Condition 4: Assumes 90 percent adoption rate, machine capacity of 700 cartons per hour, a working year or 2,240 hours.

annually will make the transition. This would account for 90 percent of production and yields a displacement rate of 83 percent. The fourth projection assumes a machine capacity of 700 cartons per hour and a work year of 2,240 hours; the first figure on expanded machine capacity has been provided by Paul Adrian, developer of the USDA Salinas prototype; the second figure on the number of hours worked per year is drawn from Johnson and Zahara. These assumptions yield a displacement rate of 88.9 percent. All our calculations have been made on the assumption of a production level of 100,000,000 cartons annually. Details on calculations are provided in Appendix 1.

The effects of technological change are not limited, however, to the workers immediately affected. It is clear that some workers, numbers and types as yet unspecified, will be required to build the harvesting machines. These workers will not be agricultural employees but will be employed by firms involved in farm equipment manufacturing. The character of the work involved will be very different from that performed by lettuce harvesters and the prospects for retraining harvest workers for new employment in equipment manufacturing will be poor.

In addition, once the machines are built and in service, some workers will be required for repair and servicing. Here the prospects for a few lettuce harvesters is somewhat improved. Repairing is a high level skill and it is unlikely that many lettuce harvesters will be able to make this transition. Servicing work, however, is an intermediate skill and some lettuce workers may possibly be retrained for this occupation.

Therefore some jobs will be created that will partially offset those lost through mechanization displacement, although we cannot estimate the overall volume of this employment. We can better estimate the prospects for retraining harvesters for servicing activities; even at the rate of one person per machine, an estimate that is extremely high, only 50 to 150 jobs will be created.

This analysis raises general questions about the long-range effects of technological innovation. An optimistic view of the process has been expressed by the vice-president of Agricultural Sciences of the University of California:

there is ample evidence to show that the very serious problem of unemployment is alleviated more by expansion than by restriction of technological innovation.

Introduction of the tomato harvester did, in the short run, reduce labor requirements. . . . When the expansion of processing, transportation, and other activities associated with this increased production is considered, total employment in this industry has increased. Moreover, one of the most physically debilitating stoop-labor tasks was eliminated . . .

Technical innovation in all industries has been accompanied by an expansion of job opportunities in the total economy (Kendrick 1977).

This view is, perhaps, overoptimistic because it pays little attention to either the growth of population or the character of demand, or most important, to the individuals specifically impacted who are unlikely to have sufficient preparation to move into new employment areas because of nontransferability of skills.

A very different view is expressed by *lechugeros* (lettuce harvesters) when asked to talk about the prospects of mechanization. In one meeting with a group of workers, this issue was raised: How did lechugeros feel about being relieved of the debilitating stoop-labor involved in their work?

Initially, workers expressed difficulties in answering this question because the answer was so obvious. A worker pointed out that they had come to the United States from Mexico to seek work. They had no preparation or skills other than for manual labor. They had no education, no English. Mechanization not only removed their *jobs;* it also displaced their wives and their children. Workers saw their children being prepared by the schools for jobs such as they themselves filled; yet these very jobs were disappearing through mechanization.

This worker, after being supported by other lechugeros, pointed out that, in tomato harvest mechanization, skilled educated workers survived the transition; it was the ones with the mechanical skills who could find jobs. The others were pushed out. As far as he was concerned, he would rather work than be displaced, even if he had to work for lower wages. These views were endorsed by the other harvesters. The sentiments of those immediately affected by mechanization are startlingly different from those unaffected by it and shielded by economic security.

Although the numbers of workers involved in lettuce is very different from the massive changes that occurred in cotton mechanization (Street 1957), on a small scale, the transition to mechanized lettuce harvesting will have similar consequences. The assessment made of technological change in nonagricultural industries many years ago still has validity, "Prospective technological changes will continue to reduce the proportion of jobs involving primarily physical and manual ability and to increase the number of jobs requiring ability to work with data and information" (U.S. Department of Labor 1966, p.9).

The advice given at that time is still sound but experience has created considerable cynicism because of programmatic failures, "This study indicates the inevitability and persuasiveness of technological change and underscores the importance of developing adequate plans to facilitate manpower adjustment" (U.S. Department of Labor 1966, p.9).

Consequences for workers: the changing labor force

Displacement represents one consequence about which varying estimates and assumptions are possible, creating considerable discussion. A second set of consequences concerning the changing characteristics of the labor force is probably more definitive. An assessment of the current labor force yields clear notions of the differences in characteristics between the ground pack and wrap pack harvesters.

Ground pack harvesters are almost entirely Mexican by origin and almost entirely male except for a small number of female "water boys." There is agreement that most harvesters are Mexican nationals; some are "green-carders," that is, citizens of Mexico with rights to legal residence in the United States. Others, and no one knows how many or what percentage they constitute, are *sindocumentos,* Mexican nationals who have entered the United States without documents. Many lechugeros maintain their families on the Mexican side of the border, commuting on a daily basis into the United States during the winter lettuce season and then moving in groups to Salinas, or other locations more distant from the border, for other seasons. From these more distant locations, they make occasional weekend trips to Mexico to join their families. An increasing number, size unknown, have settled in the Salinas area and moved their families there. In such circumstances, many Salinas-based workers follow the season south and visit their families in Salinas on occasional weekends. There are indications that some of the Salinas-based workers are becoming reluctant to "follow the loop" into the winter lettuce areas but this evidence is fragmentary.

Wrap pack harvesters are more heterogeneous in character. On the wrap machines, three basic jobs exist: cutters and lifters (who cut, trim, and elevate the lettuce to the machine), wrappers (who wrap the lettuce in film), and packers (who pack the lettuce in cartons, assemble, and close cartons). Although some movement occurs among personnel as a result of absences, cutting and trimming is predominantly a male occupation; wrapping is predominantly female; and packing is almost entirely male. Ethnically, people of Mexican extraction predominate but occasionally there are Anglos and Blacks. Many wrappers are local women who work seasonally in a particular locality; that is, they do not follow the loop. Some cutters may follow the loop but we believe that packers are the most likely of the three occupations to follow the season to other locations.

A major structural shift likely in the transition to mechanized harvesting will be from male to female. Assuming the six-person configuration of a harvest labor crew of a harvester driver, one forklift driver, two inspector-trimmers, and two inspector-loaders, we expect that the drivers will be male and the remaining workers will be predominantly female because the activities involving inspection, trimming, and loading will not be very heavy and will be machine controlled. Machne-controlled work is usually paid by the hour rather than on an incentive basis. This factor will probably also contribute to the shift from the male, incentive-oriented workers presently involved in harvesting. On this basis the structural characteristics of the harvest labor force would shift from its present overwhelming male dominance to one in which females would predominate. In other words, we expect lettuce growers to follow a strategy similar to that pursued by tomato producers.

Ground pack lettuce workers are paid on the basis of a group incentive; wrap lettuce workers are usually paid on an hourly basis. Group incentives make sense in circumstances where the work pace is controlled by the workers; where the pace is machine controlled, employers typically remunerate workers by the hour. In mechanized lettuce harvesting the work process will resemble the assembly-line type of operation found in wrap packing more than that found in ground packing. Accordingly, there is a strong likelihood that employees on the machines will be paid on an hourly basis. There is considerable probability that hourly rates will be fairly high (compared to other forms of agricultural labor) because the relationship of labor to capital investment and the value of the crop will be low. This relationship may also make it worthwhile for employers to continue to remunerate crews on some form of production basis, that is, a group incentive over and above some norm of production.

What is fairly certain, however, is that the rates of pay will be definitely lower than those earned by ground pack lettuce harvesters through the current incentive system. One consequence that can, therefore, be projected is that a number of workers accustomed to the high incentive rates will drop out of lettuce employment; some will return to Mexico, whereas others may seek nonagricultural employment in the United States. We see this happening to longtime workers in the lettuce industry rather than to new workers. Thus our general expectation is: The longer the period in the industry, the greater the probability of dropping out and returning to Mexico. Our reasoning is that the longer someone has been involved in lettuce production, the closer that person is to "burn out" and to have accumulated sufficient capital to move into another area of economic activity. Also, the longer a person is in the industry, the less willing he or she will be to work under machine-controlled conditions where employer supervision becomes much more important than in the presently self-regulating crews.

Workers on wrap machines, in contrast, will probably be more willing to make the transition to mechanized harvesting. Most are already accustomed to machine pacing and to being paid by the hour rather than on an incentive basis. Among these workers, we would anticipate that those employed in cutting and wrapping will adapt to mechanization with greater facility than closers and packers. The latter are paid higher rates[5] and probably regard themselves as having higher status. Wrappers, boxers, and loaders may feel the decline in their status more and therefore have more of a tendency to withdraw from the industry.

In summary, the consequences for the labor force should be to produce a shift toward female labor and a tendency for green-card male harvesters involved in ground packing and who follow the loop to drop out of production.

Consequences for workers: changes in work organization

Three potential sets of consequences from changes in work organization can be envisioned for workers. First, we anticipate a tendency toward internalization of the harvest labor force; that is, workers will tend to become permanent employees of specific firms whether or not they follow the loop. Second, there are strong but uncertain prospects that preharvest work, as presently constituted, will diminish but that remaining preharvest workers will be internalized to firms. Finally, we expect that sharp differences will develop in the way in which work is organized.

Internalization of lettuce harvesters

Until recently, harvest workers were almost entirely external to the lettuce firms. Unlike internalized workers who have distinctive rights and responsibilities established over time (i.e., permanent employment), lettuce harvesters typically have been outside individual firms, having few rights beyond immediate employment. In this respect, lettuce harvesters have been similar to most other agricultural workers.

Currently, contrary tendencies have developed in agriculture and particularly in the lettuce industry as a process of internalization has gotten under way. In California, Florida, and Texas where large-scale production of fruits and vegetables are common, it became necessary to internalize a segment of the labor force involved in control and maintenance operations (supervisors, office personnel, salespersons, repair persons, etc.). Other occupations have also become internalized in large operations, including drivers and servicing workers. Increased capitalization and size are factors leading to increased internalization.

Another factor contributing to internalization has been the growth of unionism in agriculture, whether that of the United Farm Workers Union or that of the Teamsters (who have withdrawn from organizing field-workers). Unions demand regularization of employment relationships, in particular, the establishment of seniority rights, with a concomitant internalization of workers.

In lettuce, where unionism began among harvesters in 1971, there has been a marked internalization of workers. Although the degree of internalization is unclear because it varies from firm to firm, the development of a mechanized harvesting system will lead to further internalization. This would be true even if unionism were to disappear from the industry, an unlikely eventuality. The reasoning behind this projection is based on the fact that the numbers of workers to be involved in lettuce harvesting under mechanized conditions will be very small. Remaining workers can be relatively well paid because their labor will constitute a small percentage of production costs. The requirement for regularity and predictability will be extremely important for it remains essential that harvesting operate with no delays. Under these circumstances, firms will find it advisable to vest workers' rights within the firm rather than to leave them to the kind of haphazard employment relationships of the past.

Internalization of preharvest workers

The condition of preharvest workers is somewhat different. Although preharvest activities involve many operations including bed formation, planting, irrigation, and the like, we are concerned here only with thinning, hoeing, and weeding. Most other preharvest activities are capital intensive but thinning-hoeing-weeding (THW) is labor intensive. THW activities are often, but not always, conducted by crews of workers employed by external labor contractors who are paid on an acreage basis at so many dollars per acre. Contractors recruit temporary workers through their own networks and supervise, transport, and pay them.

Mechanization could affect preharvest activities if the experiments in greenhouse production of seedlings and their transplantation undertaken by Bud Antle prove successful. The transplanting system affects THW activities, for the application of herbicides *before* planting eliminates the need for weeding. Because transplantation is machine controlled by individual placement of plants, the need for thinning is also eliminated. Thus the system will have effects not only on harvesting, by producing greater uniformity in the crop and predictability about maturation, but will affect preharvest workers as well. Rather than employing temporary crews of THW workers through contractors, lettuce firms will be able to organize greenhouse production on a year-round basis. Seedlings can be transported from central growing places to any production location within twenty-four hours. The success of this system would be encouraged by the transition to harvest mechanization and accelerate the process by which preharvest workers are internalized into the lettuce firms.

A secondary effect will be experienced by labor contractors because they will no longer be required to recruit THW crews for lettuce. This does not necessarily mean that contractors will be eliminated because they are employed for THW activities in crops other than lettuce and often harvest other crops. However, it will affect their income possibilities and marginal contractors may be unable to survive. Another secondary effect would be experienced by the seasonal workers employed by contractors in THW operations. They would also find work potential dropping and their income affected. The numbers involved and the magnitude of the consequences are difficult to estimate.

Yet another secondary effect may be experienced in the relations between the two unions involved in lettuce production and distribution, the United Farm Workers Union (UFW) and the Teamsters Union. Fieldwork is accepted as being within UFW jurisdiction, whereas work inside sheds and greenhouses is covered by the Teamsters. With the seedlings system, THW activities will decrease or be eliminated and replaced by greenhouse and transplantational activities. Thus a shift in jurisdictional coverage will have to be confronted by the unions involved. Given the history of tensions between the two unions, the only possible reliable estimate is that such a transition will create interorganizational problems.

Work organization

On the mechanized harvester, work will be organized in a way that more closely resembles the work process on wrap machines than that found in ground packing. Work will be machine paced with the key controlling factor being the driver of the machine. On the machine itself, we anticipate a reduction in differences between workers (except for the driver and forklift operator). We see the activities of inspection, trimming, and packing as involving easily translatable skills and therefore expect that workers will often exchange jobs on a voluntary basis, particularly to relieve boredom.

In this respect, the pattern of work organization more closely resembles the patterns found on tomato harvesting machines (before the introduction of the electronic sorter). Here there were two basic job categories: drivers and sorters. In such circumstances, self-regulation with respect to the work process becomes very important. On the tomato harvester, for example, some positions were preferred more than others. These differences were handled, in some crews, by rotating job positions during the day. Whether rotation occurs depended more on workers and on the basis for the crew organization than on employers who were relatively indifferent to the problems involved. Where crews were largely recruited through crew members, through kinship and friendship networks, rotation became a common feature. On other crews where members were individually hired by the employer, there was no such basis for rotation and an experienced family might protect itself by grabbing the best positions on the belts and refusing to move.

This eventuality appears less likely in lettuce. Mechanized crews will not ony be smaller but lettuce growers have had more experience with workers and work organization than tomato growers. The presence of unionism will also encourage the development of equitability in work organization *as long as pay differentials do not exist*. Thus we can anticipate a tendency toward work rotation, toward crew homogeneity and identity, by harvest workers. The same will be true, although to a lesser extent, with preharvest workers who will form stable social relationships with fellow employees where they are in daily contact.

A secondary effect of changes in work organization, as noted with respect to the seedlings procedures, may be to create jurisdictional problems between the Teamsters and the UFW concerning workers on the harvest machine. Teamsters normally claim jurisdiction over "anything on wheels" whereas the UFW has jurisdiction over field-workers. The utilization of what is essentially a mobile factory on wheels operating in the fields can, therefore, be expected to create problems requiring jurisdictional settlement between the two unions.

Community consequences: housing, schools, social services

Two fundamental possibilities exist with respect to the harvest labor force following mechanization: (1) maintenance of mobility, "following the loop" or (2) development of stability – working the season in a particular locality on a full-time basis and engaging in other activities or withdrawal from employment after the season ends. These activities could include: employment with the same employer or another employer in other work, finding different employment, drawing unemployment compensation benefits, withdrawal from the labor force. The alternatives are presented diagrammatically in Figure 4.1.

In contrast to our expectations with respect to the rate of adoption of the machine by grower-shippers, we expect the response of workers to their potential alternatives to be more heterogeneous. From the viewpoint of employers, mobility of workers may be preferable to stability because they could then depend upon a single experienced labor force. In contrast, a stabilized work force will require reassembly and retraining at the beginning of the season at each location. The construction of a mobile labor force with a heavily female component will involve many complex

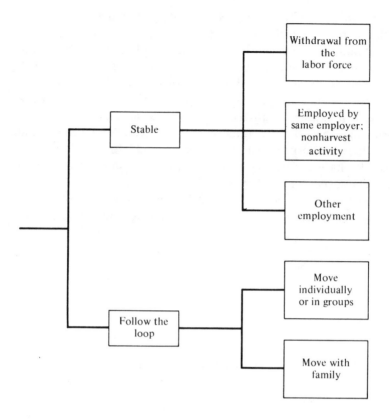

Figure 4.1   Stability–mobility options of lettuce workers

social impacts. For example, because women bear the burdens of family more immediately than men, women tend to be less mobile than men. A migratory labor force could be constructed from women in pre- and post-marital and familial situations but might be marked by considerable instability because workers in such a situation, male or female, are less stable in employment than workers with families. Some employers may seek to resolve the character of their labor force by maintaining mobile males (working as drivers and forklift operators) and stable females (as inspectors, trimmers, loaders).

Whether mobile or stable, the internalization of workers projected earlier will have the consequences of making employment in lettuce more of a "career" than it is now, that is, a set of activities that is carried on for a lifetime or, at least, for a considerable period of one's life. In this respect, mechanical harvesting may change the view of the harvesters from that, at present, of considering work in lettuce as something one does to accumulate funds to pursue a "career" outside lettuce after a decade or so involved in harvesting.

Workers who look upon employment as a career rather than for a short period function with respect to everyday life differently from those who regard their employment as temporary. They know that they will be recalled to work; that work will be conducted for fairly specific periods of time; that remuneration will be predictable; and that certain economic benefits accrue and accumulate. Under these circumstances, workers typically make plans with respect to expenditures: It becomes feasible to plan housing, to develop long-range plans about daily life such as when to purchase large appliances, as well as to make plans and to develop expectations with respect to children. Accordingly, we project that lettuce harvesters will develop clearer and more definitive expectations with respect to housing, education, and social services.

Expectations will develop, as well, with respect to consumption generally but we anticipate fewer secondary consequences as a result. One projection, for example, is that with regularized and improved incomes, the character of food consumption will change, with more of a tendency to purchase meat and prepared foods. This can lead to an upgrading of food supplies at markets that regularly serve such workers, or the opening of new markets serving this new custom. The impact of such changes, however, will have little social impact beyond what can be termed "ripple" effects.

Ripple effects may be present with respect to other expenditures. Lettuce workers may want to upgrade transportation by buying newer cars or purchasing them more frequently. This may have minor effects on automobile dealers, some of whom may be interested in the employment of Chicano salespersons in the hope of attracting potential purchasers. Thus some new employment may develop for people from the same ethnic group as lettuce workers, but it is somewhat unlikely that this employment will draw displaced workers. Similar ripple effects can be expected with the sale of major and minor appliances; the numbers sold to lettuce workers may increase but it will not affect the distribution and sales network significantly.

In contrast we anticipate more profound effects in three areas: housing, education, and social services.

Housing

If work is stable, the augmentation and regularization of income will lead workers to begin to improve their housing conditions. Most agricultural workers live in poor housing. With regularized incomes, workers can be expected to plan housing expenditures through home purchase or improvement. Home improvement will have ripple effects as most work will be done by family members, friends, or small contractors; the purchase of materials will be effected through existing distribution networks and will not produce any important changes.

The purchase of new houses, however, will have significant effects, especially if lettuce workers enter the housing market in substantial numbers. Thus we anticipate the effects of lettuce mechanization on housing in the Salinas Valley, and proximate areas, to be noticeable for several years after the transition. The Salinas Valley is a relatively encapsulated geographical and social system: Although people can commute in and out, it is relatively difficult, and most agricultural workers working in the valley also live in it. If several hundred workers purchase houses for the first time or improve their housing by purchasing better housing, there will be some impact on the housing market.

The probabilities are that housing in a restricted price range will be impacted; because housing prices are highly volatile, we can only estimate the value range in terms of current (1980) dollar values. Our expectations are that the impacted housing stock will be in the lower-income housing range appropriate to situations in which the husband is a regular full-time, year-round employee, and the wife can work for half a year or more annually. We estimate this at $60,000 to 80,000 at 1980 housing costs for the area.

Assessments of the effects of harvest mechanization on the housing market must be severely qualified because the expansion of the metropolitan San Jose area to the south, that is, toward Salinas, has already had some impact on housing prices. The volatility of housing and credit markets in the past five years also must be noted. These effects on Salinas housing will unquestionably be more profound than the impact of the settlement and upgrading of housing of some hundreds of lettuce worker families.

For mobile workers following the loop, we anticipate a tendency to deal with their situation in two ways: Workers will either move with their families or without them. In cases of workers moving without families, we can expect that present arrangements will prevail in which workers find temporary housing when they are working the season away from family

locations. If workers move with their families, they may begin to resemble mobile heavy construction workers in their housing arrangements.
Heavy construction workers live with great employment uncertainties
from time to time. They earn much higher wages but remain in one
location for longer periods of time than lettuce workers. They resolve
their housing and mobility requirements through mobile home and heavy
duty vehicles capable of pulling their homes. This outcome might become
more feasible for lettuce harvesting mobiles. The purchase of the homes
and vehicles would have only ripple effects; but the demand for the
construction of placement sites would be more significant. The demand
for paved sites with access to water, gas, electricity, and sewage will
create some problems. Usually the provision of power poses relatively
small problems; water provision may be more complicated in some areas;
sewage may be a much more difficult problem if local sewer facilities are
presently at peak utilization, thus preventing additional population.

Schools

Whether harvest workers remain mobile *or* become more stable, it can be
anticipated that expectations with respect to schools will change considerably. Although education has already become more important for many
harvest workers, as their employment stabilizes expectations about their
children's educations will increase. When people experience greater predictability in their life circumstances, they begin to consider means by
which "investments" in children can be maximized in terms of the real
and symbolic opportunities in the larger society. Although most parents
coming from poor economic circumstances have hopes for their children,
when life is unpredictable and vicarious, few plans can be made. As life
becomes more predictable, parents begin to think of their children fitting
into the mainstream of the social order. As long as lechugeros maintain
homes in Mexico, think of lettuce harvesting as a young person's means
to accumulate funds to use at a later period for a different "career,"
educational expectations remain uncertain. As lettuce harvesters become
more regular employees, they will manifest the same expectations as
other parents who share similar life circumstances.

Thus we anticipate the creation of new constituencies in several school
systems where lettuce workers can be expected to concentrate and the
formulation, over a period of time, of new demands on the school systems. The school districts that can be expected to be particularly impacted will be in the Salinas Valley and Watsonville area.

Parents will become increasingly sensitive to the way teachers interact with their children, particularly their ethnicity; to demand higher quality teaching; to insist upon more interaction with the school system. If parents move into upgraded housing, it can be anticipated that children of Mexican extraction will appear in greater numbers in schools that have been largely Anglo in character. Parents with stabilized incomes can be expected to manifest characteristics commonly associated, in the U.S. context, with being "middle class."

For mobile workers who move with their families, it can be expected that there will be increasing pressure for the efficient handling and transfer of records of children's education between school systems and for greater coordination between school systems so that children's school lives are less disrupted.

Parents will probably begin a slow entry into the political network surrounding the schools, initially in the parent–teacher associations, but subsequently developing interest in school politics. Although most lechugeros are not citizens and therefore unable to participate in electing school boards, stabilization in employment should produce a shift to U.S. citizenship and the beginning of participation in political activities surrounding schooling. Many workers will experience a variety of pressures through unions and ethnic associations to become citizens and active in political life. It is very often through problems and grievances over the education of children that political action becomes meaningful; political life at the state and national levels is too distant. Thus we anticipate the school systems to become a fertile area through which political participation and involvement will manifest after the transition to mechanized harvesting and the stabilization of employment.

Social services

Expectations with respect to social services, and consequent increases in demand for services, can be expected to increase with the transition to mechanization. Among these services to be impacted will be unemployment compensation and health, in particular.

Unemployment compensation facilities will be impacted because regularization of employment leads to greater demand: When workers are marginalized, their expectations about services from the state are also marginal. They know from experience that they have only marginal rights, that administrators and functionaries shuffle them around, and so on. When workers become stable in employment, when organizations such as unions inform them systematically about their rights and create service support systems, the demand for services is expected to increase. Thus we expect that lettuce workers who experience unemployment will become more regular clients of employment compensation offices in California and Arizona, particularly in the Salinas and Imperial valleys and environs.

Health also constitutes an area of greater expectation. As workers become regularized, working conditions such as health insurance, hospitalization insurance, sick leave, and so on become a normal part of their lives. With regular employment and predictable income, it is rational to protect one's health. Therefore we project an increase in demand for health services, particularly in the Salinas Valley. Much of this demand will shift to private physicians and/or perhaps encourage the development of group private practice specifically geared to the client population of stably employed agricultural workers. An increase in hospital services, laboratory services, and auxiliary and associated health activities can also be expected. Most of these demands will constitute only ripple effects and will not be especially notable. Public agencies concerned with health care can be expected to be somewhat impacted because of higher demand. If these demands are not planned for, we anticipate increasing political involvement and participation around issues of public policy and health at the county level somewhat similar to that discussed with respect to schools.

Community consequences: the Imperial Valley and Baja California

Most of our projections thus far have focused on the Salinas Valley, the prime lettuce-producing area in the California–Arizona lettuce production system. The Salinas Valley has the longest production season, matched only by the Santa Maria season which is longer but where production constitutes approximately 25 percent of Salinas. The Imperial Valley season lasts about four to five months and volume is just slightly more than 50 percent that of Salinas. Other districts have seasons of varying lengths but are of less significance than the two prime producing districts, Salinas and Imperial. We now turn to a consideration of the consequences that can be expected in the border area, the Imperial Valley in California and the Baja California area in Mexico.

Workers continuing to make their base in the border area can be anticipated to continue to retain their homes in Mexico rather than in the

United States. For this reason we foresee fewer impacts on the Imperial Valley than on Mexico from these workers. The one major exception that can be projected would be with a system of harvesting based on mobile workers, as previously noted. In such circumstances, there will be a sharp increase in demand for mobile home sites in the Imperial Valley with concomitant demand for water, electricity, and sewage. This could create problems in some areas of the Imperial Valley where sewage systems are reported as being at capacity. Therefore it can be anticipated that local authorities will experience pressure for the development of infrastructural facilities. These pressures will originate as much (if not more) from employers as from workers because grower-shippers, under such conditions, will want to ensure the stability of their labor force.

More significant impacts can be anticipated on the Mexican side of the border, particularly in the cities of Mexicali and San Luis. Mexicali is especially notable, to the extent that we can assess location without a survey or census, as the residential location of most lechugeros.

In the past, when lechugeros withdrew from the industry, settled into new occupations or returned to their "home" areas, this tended to be individual movement and its impact was negligible. The transition to mechanization can be expected to have an impact that will be felt on a sizable number of workers within a relatively short time. Thus, from the estimates provided in Table 4.3, the number could be as small as 360 workers (or less) over a five-year period or as much as 5,000 workers (or more) within three years.

The *municipio* of Mexicali is a sizable city whose population now probably exceeds 400,000. Even with maximum displacement of workers, the overall effects of a transition to mechanization will not be experienced as a serious dislocation in the municipio of Mexicali because the most serious eventuality would have an effect on only 1.25 percent of Mexicali's population (5000/400,000 = 1.25 percent). If one considers, however, the impact on the economically active population of 99,381 or the male economically active population of 77,303 (Gobierno del Estado de Baja California Norte: Table 1.2), the maximum estimate on displacement would constitute 5 and 6.47 percent, respectively. The impact of such numbers on Mexicali would be more significant.

The impact on the Mexicali municipio will be greater than the impact on the potential number of jobs lost. Each lettuce worker usually has a dependent family. Thus the effects on family dependents, although not measurable, cannot simply be dismissed. Similarly, each worker domiciled in Mexicali presently has a multiplier effect on the local economy because workers' needs are supplied by food retailers, other retail shops, and the like. As employment declines as a result of the transition to mechanized harvesting, Mexicali can expect to experience a *divider* effect; that is, for each job lost by a lettuce worker, there will be a number of jobs lost in the local economy. Again, although not measurable, the loss of employment by lechugeros will have effects on the Mexicali economy.

Not all ground pack harvesters, it must be noted, live in the Mexicali municipio. Some live in the San Luis municipio in Baja California and some live in the Imperial Valley and/or the Yuma, Arizona areas. We justify our use of the Mexicali figures on the basis of our belief that the overwhelming bulk of lechugeros living in the border area actually make their residences in Mexicali.

The social impact on the Mexicali area, we anticipate, will not be so significant as the impact to be experienced within the United States. First, the system of infrastructural benefits for workers is different in Mexico from what it is in the United States, resulting in different expectations. Second, workers withdrawing from the industry will, we expect, be those who have been in it longest and who, therefore, have the greater reserves to make a transition to another form of economic activity. Such workers can be anticipated to shift into small-scale trading, driving, agriculture, and possibly small-scale real estate development. Although the numbers making this transition can be sizable and will constitute a "surge," in contrast to the individual transitions that have occurred in the past, we foresee only ripple effects in Baja California. However, we should note that our research has been concentrated within the United States and that the examination of effects on Baja California have been somewhat cursory. Additional examination of this subject by someone on the Mexican side of the border would be valuable.

5. Conclusion

In the course of this study we have presented a number of theoretical, methodological, and empirical issues. This final chapter is aimed at drawing together the findings and the implications of the case study into a concluding statement related to the sociology of agriculture and the comparative analysis of production systems.

The determinants of technological change in production: lessons from the lettuce and tomato studies

The empirical examination of the lettuce industry occurred after the setting of fairly specific research questions that focused on the factors affecting technological change as discussed in Chapter 1. These questions derived from three basic sources:

1. Dissatisfaction with the tendency toward a notion of almost unilinear technological change found in much of the Marxist literature on the labor process.
2. Disagreement with a technological determinist view of change in production systems.
3. The belief that agriculture operates in a similar fashion to other production systems despite the lack of attention paid to agriculture by either rural or industrial sociology.

We are now in a position to elaborate on the model of technological change presented earlier and to use it to explain the different findings in the lettuce and tomato studies. For purposes of reference, we repeat Figure 1.1 but note that a double-headed arrow has been added to suggest an interactive relationship between the two independent variables. The changed figure is represented in Figure 5.1.

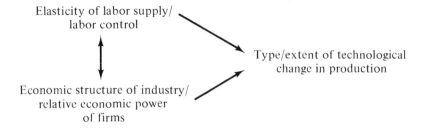

Figure 5.1 Revised causal model of technological change

The model elaborated

Three major assertions are encompassed in the model:

1. Labor supply and control is a critical independent variable in the examination of work organization in all production systems and has been especially important in agriculture in both of the empirical examples presented. Because the availability of an appropriate labor supply is critical to the survival of each industry, fluctuations in this variable will have significant and direct influence on the type or extent of technological change expected.

2. Range of choices of new technologies will be greatly influenced by the economic organization of the industry and the relative power of the individual firms in the industry.

3. Differential outcomes, in terms of technological change, resulting from change in the labor supply/control variable, will also be influenced by the interactive effect of the economic organization and the labor supply/control variables. That is, the manner in which firms perceive or anticipate change in labor supply/control will be influenced by their economic strength. Thus strategies with respect to technological change will also be influenced by the interaction of these independent variables.

Before undertaking an explanation of the technological change in our empirical cases, let us briefly elaborate on the variable representing economic structure.

Part of the rationale for choosing lettuce and tomatoes for comparative analysis, as indicated earlier, was the differential response in each production system to what was viewed as a critical historical change in the organization of the agricultural labor market: the end of the bracero program. An additional factor in the formulation of the responses in each system, we argue, is the differential economic organization of the industries. Although we risk redundancy in our argument, it is essential that clarity be maintained as to how the industries rank differently on the economic structure variable. Stated briefly, producing firms in the tomato industry have historically been weak agents in dealing with processors. Particularly before mechanization, these firms (or farms) operated on a seasonal basis with a strategy of short-term profit maximization. That is, although firms did not necessarily stake their economic survival on the tomato crop alone, neither did they move in the direction of expansion or integration into processing. In large part, this was because such avenues were closed to them by the oligopolistic position of the processors. Thus, with respect to processors, producer firms constituted a relatively weak and manipulable set of forces.

In the lettuce industry, by contrast, the integration of producers and marketers occurred fairly early. The combination of production and marketing enabled grower-shippers to move toward stable, year-round production and long-term profit maximization. Grower-shippers were, therefore, in a position to innovate in production practices, to expand and diversify their crops and, at the same time, attract capital and financing from sources outside agriculture. As described in Chapter 3, the resources of companies such as Dow Chemical and Castle and Cooke have proven extremely important for the continued growth of the Antle Company; similarly, United Brands has provided the capital necessary for the expansion of Sun Harvest. Thus two important differences arise immediately when comparing the firms producing lettuce and tomatoes: (1) the greater capacity for innovation and cost absorption for lettuce grower-shippers and the relative dependence of tomato producers and (2) the establishment, by the grower-shippers, of processorlike hegemony in the lettuce industry.

We can now turn to a consideration of the causal linkages of the model. Summarizing the argument, we will contend that the supply and control of the labor factor influences the type of technological change developed and that firms will use technological change to improve their economic position.

Labor supply/control and technological change

The degree of magnitude of change in the supply or control of the labor factor will greatly influence the type of technological change adopted by an industry. Although, as has been suggested, there is an interactive effect between labor and the economic structure variables, when change in the labor factor becomes imminent, action in the direction of techno-logical change will be taken to ensure the survival of the industry.

In the tomato industry the end of the bracero program appeared catas-trophic and led to an immediate change in the technology of production. But because of the centrality of cheap and controllable labor, and the dependence of producers on the labor supply, the change in production technology had to be of transformational magnitude. That is, in order to achieve a *drastic* reduction in the demand for labor, the entire production system had to be transformed to achieve considerable efficiencies over the previous labor system. The creation of this new system, however, simultaneously and necessarily outmoded many auxiliary activities in pro-duction. The 60-pound lug box, for example, was appropriate for condi-tions of labor surplus but was ridiculously undersized for the machine harvest system. The magnitude of change in harvest technology, a result of the former centrality of cheap labor, therefore, precipitated a transfor-mation of the entire production system.

In lettuce, in contrast, the demise of the bracero program was not perceived as such a catastrophic threat. Grower-shippers did experiment with alternative forms of work organization in response to the unsettling of the labor market. However, economic survival was not deemed as problematic in lettuce despite the importance of bracero workers. Grower-shippers had an economic cushion not available to the more de-pendent tomato growers; they were geared toward long-term profit max-imization and were in a better position to absorb cost increases or to pass them along to consumers. Rather than rush to mechanization, lettuce firms bid up the price of labor sufficiently to attract enough workers, citizens, green-carders, or undocumented workers. The cushion provided by their economic position enabled the grower-shippers to ride out the crisis period in the labor market – until such time as it became clear that green-carders and undocumented workers were and would continue to be available.

We are not suggesting that the lettuce industry was or is insensitive to changes in labor supply and control. Rather, we argue that the economic organization of the industry has made it possible to respond to the labor factor with incremental changes in technology rather than with transfor-mational ones. Thus we view the introduction of wrap machine harvesting as an incremental response to the industry's desire to decrease uncer-tainty in the supply of labor, to increase control over production via machine pacing and rationalization, and to attempt to offset organizational advances by farm worker unions (especially the UFW).

It is primarily in connection with this last aspect of labor supply/control – unionization – that we have been most concerned. We suggested in our projection of the conditions under which mechanization will occur that the sustained growth of unionism in lettuce will make the mechanization alternative more attractive to grower-shippers. Although mechanization may also be spurred by innovations in handling technology, in either case, the magnitude of technological change in the totality of the production system will be transformational. That is, the continued struggle for control over labor supply and work conditions will constitute the functional equivalent in the lettuce industry of the end of the bracero program for the tomato industry.

Firms, technological change, and economic position

Firms in an industry may act on the technological organization of the labor process in such a way as to improve their economic position. This suggests, as demonstrated by the Antle company case, that firms can have an independent effect on the state of production technology. Antle, it will be recalled, has undertaken numerous innovations on seedlings, cooling, wrapping, packing, and transport, both to economize and to enhance its market position. A more general case involves a further explanation of the lettuce wrapping machine. Wrapping, although having definite and important effects on labor supply and control, also provides companies with the opportunity to begin to establish brand name identification.

As might be expected, and as has been demonstrated in this case study, these changes have been, on the whole, incremental in character. They have not affected the totality of the production system but, instead, have been oriented toward limited segments. This, we suggest, is a result of the costs and risks transformational changes might have for the individual firms. Equally important, there has been no substantive need for individual firms to respond to particularized problems of labor supply and control, for example, extremely long strikes or harassment of illegals by the Border Patrol. Nonetheless, it is conceivable that a strategy of expensive incremental change can be adopted by some firms capable of "upping the ante" for staying in business, that is, forcing less financially endowed companies out of competition.

An unexplored avenue in both case studies is how the parameters of technological innovations are determined. That is, we can observe empirically that concentration of production accompanied mechanization in to-matoes and have attempted to explain how this has occurred. Similarly, we have projected increased concentration in lettuce with harvest mech-anization. This latter projection has been informed by the design and the estimated costs of the harvesting machines. The question that has not been considered, but which deserves exploration, is the influence exerted within the industry on the cost, functions, and capacity of the machine. That is, taking the transition to mechanized harvesting as a given, how are these parameters communicated to the research and development network responsible for design? Why, for example, were tomato harvest-ing machines put together in such a way as to "require" certain acreages in order to prove them economically efficient? As we will argue in the concluding section, these are important issues to be considered in future studies in the sociology of agriculture.

The model, as already presented and elaborated in the case study, incorporates the major thrust of recent works on the labor process and the sensitivity to organizational response to change. Referring again to Burawoy (1979) and Noble (1978), we have demonstrated through em-pirical and historical data that: (1) changes in the supply or control over labor precipitate efforts on the part of capitalist organizations to minimize dependence on political power through reorganization of production and (2) even when "appropriate" or acceptable labor-saving technologies are available, firms will not necessarily adopt them if alternative, but not necessarily less expensive, production systems provide equivalent results.

These conclusions argue against both the theory of working class ho-mogenization and technological determinism. The analysis of political power exercised by firms in the labor market (directly and through the state) points up the heterogeneity of working class composition (e.g., citizen vs. noncitizen) and the substitution of segments of the working class for one another (e.g., women used to displace men). The analysis of the factors influencing the rate and direction of technological change argue quite strongly against a unilinear progression of scientific research.

It is, nonetheless, clear that the model we have set out remains to be tested and refined rigorously. In this sense, much can be gained from parallel work carried out by organizational theorists and analysts (Thompson 1967; Perrow 1968; Aldrich 1979; and Chandler 1969, among others). Although the model presented in this book lacks the sophistica-tion of this other work, three summary comments can be derived from our formulations: (1) The sort of attempt we have undertaken at macro-structural analysis has not previously been carried out with respect to the major agricultural industries in the United States; (2) we have argued that researchers ought to be sensitive to the social factors determining the range or extent of technological change, as opposed to the more economic models of market determination; and (3) we have stressed the importance of power relations between organizations within industries as affecting technological change.[1]

Directions for a sociology of agriculture and the comparative analysis of production systems

Recapitulating briefly, this research has been aimed at the extension of two major fields of inquiry: the sociology of agriculture and the comparative analysis of production systems. As we have envisioned, the sociology of agriculture constitutes a subset of the comparative analysis. Our effort has been to elucidate the social organization of agriculture through comparative analysis of crop industries in agricultural production. The approach we have taken has not exhausted the subjects that need to be considered; some of these will be suggested subsequently. However, we attempted to bring to light the important social, political, and economic aspects of the agricultural sector; for example, growers, shippers, workers and labor organizations, and influential nonagricultural forces.

In the context of the sociology of agriculture and comparative analysis of production systems, a further attempt has been made to build an explanatory/projective model for technological change. The applicability of such a model clearly extends beyond agriculture; attention has been focused on agriculture because of its importance in the U.S. economy. Considerable change has taken place in the organization of agricultural production in the past fifty years and increases in productivity have largely been the product of increases in technological sophistication. But such advances and the source and funding of the research that provide them deserve critical analysis and discussion. The role of the state and institutional networks such as the land grant colleges must be evaluated in the light of the demise of the family farm, the displacement of hundreds of thousands of farm workers, the deterioration of food quality and nutrition, the deterioration of environment, and the increased energy demands of production in an era of energy constraints. The methodology of social projection, as presented here, has been aimed at developing an approach to anticipating those effects through the scientific analysis of production systems.

As testimony to the fact that the sociology of agriculture exists in a developmental stage, however, there remain important topics that must be integrated over time. There is insufficient space in this volume to elaborate on some of them; yet they are important enough at least to be mentioned. Research in the following issues will enable the sociology of agriculture to articulate with and draw from existing research in the more general sociology of production:

1. The comparative analysis of stratification in different production sectors in agriculture is a subject that cries for examination. Why do the production organizations in the Sunbelt (California, Arizona, Florida, Texas) take the form of agribusiness in contrast to the large, family-based, although often corporatized, farms of other places? Rural sociologists, with the fairly startling exceptions of T. Lynn Smith (1969) and Richard Rodefeld (1974), have largely ignored this subject.
2. The development of monocultural forms represents a useful opportunity for the historical analysis of agricultural production within capitalism. Going from fairly broad scale farming to monoculture within a relatively short period of time, we can better understand the historical examination of the forces pushing producers toward specialization. Some work has been done in this area by economists and some historians, but comparative analysis, particularly of a sociological character, is still lacking.
3. The varying forms of concentration in U.S. agriculture require analysis. There remains considerable debate about the continuation and viability of the family farm. The critics of the agricultural establishment have emphasized the fact that agricultural production is increasingly dominated by a handful of vertically integrated multinational corporations. Tenneco, Del Monte, Beatrice Foods, and the like are names used by the critics to indicate the entry into production of large corporate entities through backward integration. Little is known, however, other than the aggregate figures on the increased size of production units about the trends encompassed in Earl Butz's injunction to "get big or get out." One aspect of "getting bigger" is the incorporation of the family farm, a trend to which *no* attention has been given by rural sociologists. How many family farms are being incorporated and what their significance is with respect to unincorporated family farms and/or agribusiness corporate farms is simply unknown as are the effects of incorporation on the family.

4. The development of organizations and social movements within agriculture that counterpose the complex of organizations linked to the USDA and the land grant system is one major body of knowledge that has been largely ignored by sociologists although it has been examined more thoroughly by historians, with the notable exception among rural sociologists of Taylor (1952). The study of social movements, in contrast to the development of organizations of social control, constitutes an important subject area that has been largely ignored.

The extension of comparisons of production systems should, finally, entail both agricultural and nonagricultural industries. Although, in this study, we have largely restricted our analysis to agricultural industries, it is clear that the social categories of organization are fundamentally the same as in manufacturing industries despite differences in physical environments.

To echo Carey McWilliams's (1971) pioneer study in this field, there are not only "factories in the field," but they have become more pervasive and bigger.

Appendix 1. Basis for calculation of displacement numbers and rates

This appendix provides detailed reasoning for the assumptions that have been made with respect to the prospects for labor displacement. It also provides the details of arithmetic calculations. The data provided here are summarized in Table 4.3.

The Johnson – Zahara data

Johnson and Zahara (1976b) see a potential displacement of workers as a result of mechanization based on an annual adoption rate of 5 percent increasing to a total of 25 percent. They base their calculations on the assumption that there are 100 ground pack and 30 wrap pack crews. These assumptions produce the following table (Johnson and Zahara 1976b, p.330):

Table A1.1. *Displacement of Workers Resulting from Mechanization*

	5 percent rate	25 percent rate
Number of crews affected		
Of the 100 ground pack	5	25
Of the 30 wrap	1.5	7.5
Number of workers lost		
9 ground pack workers/crew	45	225
18 wrap pack workers/crew	27	135

The assumptions here are for a harvest labor force totaling 4,590, based on 100 ground pack crews of 36 workers each and 30 wrap crews of 33 workers each [(36 × 100) + (33 × 30) = 4,590]. With a 25 percent adoption rate over a five-year period, the number of displaced workers is 360, consequently the displacement rate is 7.5 percent.

139

Condition 1

The assumptions in this condition are of a labor force of 6,000 workers. The machine capacity assumed is 450 cartons per hour.

In this condition it is assumed that the larger grower-shippers, who are also the main shippers of wrapped lettuce, will be the adopters, and that the largest representing 50 percent of California–Arizona production will adopt. We make an assumption that these growers ship approximately one-third of production as wrapped lettuce. This is based on reported information that Bruce Church ships 40,000 cartons daily of which 22,400 or 56 percent are wrapped lettuce (Linden 1977b). This same source informs us that Church has 14 wrap crews of 32 people each, or 448 workers. Each wrap crew produces 1,600 cartons/day or 1,600 cartons × 14 crews = 22,400 cartons per day. Bruce Church, Inter Harvest, Bud Antle, Garin, and Finerman are notable for shipping wrapped lettuce. Thus we believe our assumption that one-third of production from the largest grower-shippers is wrapped lettuce is a conservative estimate.

We further estimate that the largest 12 grower-shippers employ only 50 percent of the labor force in a proportion of 60 percent of the workers being ground pack harvesters and the remaining 40 percent being wrap packers. Based on our assumption of a total labor force of 6,000 workers (half of which equals 3,000), this yields 1,800 ground packers and 1,200 wrap packers.

We assume that the transition, with the dozen largest grower-shippers, will be 100 percent to mechanization and to wrapped lettuce in a tube-and-cube configuration. Finally, we assume six workers are necessary to operate the harvest machine: one driver, two inspector-trimmers, two inspector-packers, and one forklift operator.

On this basis, we obtain the following calculations:

With a machine capability of operation 1,800 hours/year, the production of 50 percent of total assumed production of 100,000,000 cartons/year will require 62 machines.

> 450 cartons/hour × 1,800 hours/year = 810,000 cartons/year/machine
> 50,000,000 cartons/810,000 = 61.73 machines = 62 machines
> 62 machines × 6 workers/machine = 372 workers required to produce half of California/Arizona production
> 3,000 workers producing 50 percent of production + 372 = 3,372 total workers required

6,000 workers presently working − 3,372 working after 50 percent mechanization = 2,628 workers displaced from the industry
2,628/6,000 = 43.8 percent displacement for the total industry

Condition 2

The assumptions and calculations for this condition are identical to the previous one with the exception that we have assumed the requirement of 12 workers to staff the harvest machine, at least initially. The assumption is then applied, as in condition 1, to the 12 largest grower-shippers who ship 50 percent of production.

62 machines × 12 workers/machine = 744 workers required to produce half of California/Arizona production
3,000 workers producing 50 percent of production + 744 = 3,744 total workers required
6,000 workers presently working − 3,744 working after 50 percent mechanization = 2,256 workers displaced from the industry
2,256/6,000 = 37.6 percent displacement for the total industry

Condition 3

This condition assumes that all grower-shippers producing 500 carlots or more annually will make the transition to mechanization. Based on our assumption of total production of 100,000,000 cartons, this means that 90 percent or 90,000,000 cartons will be mechanically harvested.

To calculate the numbers of workers required to harvest this volume of lettuce, we recall that Johnson and Zahara (1976b, p.380) provided production norms of 480 cartons/hour for 36-person ground pack crews and 178 cartons/hour for 33-person wrap crews. We retain *our* estimate of a working year at 1,800 hours and our assumption that one-third of production is wrapped lettuce. This produces the following calculations:

Ground pack:

480 cartons/hour × 1,800 hours/year = 864,000 cartons/year/crew
66,000,000 cartons/864,000 = 76.4 (77) crews × 36 workers/crew = 2,722 ground pack harvesters

Wrap pack:

178 cartons/hour × 1,800 hours/year = 320,400 cartons/year/crew
33,000,000/320,400 = 103 crews × 33 workers/crew = 3,399 wrap pack workers

The total number of workers in the industry, based on this calculation would be: 2,722 ground pack harvesters + 3,399 wrap pack harvesters = 6,171 worker equivalents. Because not every worker works every day, the total number of *actual* workers will approximate something higher than 6,171. If we assume that 10 percent over the number of worker equivalents will be necessary, the total number of workers required in the industry would be 6,788 (6,171 + 617).

In this third condition we assume that *all* mechanically harvested lettuce will be wrap packed (e.g., 90 percent of production) and the remaining production will be ground packed.

90,000,000 cartons of lettuce could be harvested by 111 machine harvesting crews: 90,000,000/450 cartons/hour/machine × 1,800 hours/year = 111.1 machines. Assuming each crew is staffed with six workers, the total personnel required is 666.

The remaining 10 percent of the harvest, which would be hand harvested and ground packed would be picked by 11.6 = 12 crews × 36 workers = 432 hand harvesters.

432 hand harvesters + 666 machine harvesters = 1,098 workers total.

Assuming 6,171 workers before mechanization, the displacement rate is: 6,171 − 1098 = 5,073/6,171 = 82.2 percent displacement rate.

Assuming 6,788 workers before mechanization, the displacement rate is: 6,788 − 1,098 = 5,690/6,788 = 83.8 percent.

Effectively we consider this to be an 83 percent displacement rate.

Condition 4

Thus far we have sought to make all the conditions and assumptions with respect to the transition as conservatively as possible. The various assumptions we made have been based on present capacity of the machine, time study data based on production capabilities, and the like. The assumption of six workers is based on a belief that the technology of harvesting, trimming, wrapping, and packing can be resolved on an almost fully automated basis; this assumption we believe to be reasonable based on technological developments elsewhere in agricultural production.

In this final set of conditions, we assume two basic changes: (1) We assume a machine capacity of 700 cartons per hour. This figure is based on an assessment by Paul Adrian, developer of the Salinas prototype, as to capacity, were a two bed, four row harvester to be implemented – an idea that is technically feasible. (2) We assume, at the same time, the number of working hours is 2,240 hours per year utilizing Johnson – Zahara estimates. On this basis, utilizing all other assumptions of condition 3, we arrive at a displacement of 5,244 workers at a rate of 87.1 percent.

The basis for this condition is:

700 cartons/hour × 2,240 hours/year = 1,568,000 cartons/crew/year
90,000,000 cartons/1,568,000 = 57.4 crews = 58 crews
58 × 6 workers = 348 workers for 90 percent of the harvest
348 + 432 unimpacted hand harvesters = 780 workers remaining in the industry

Assume 6,000 or 7,000 workers in the industry at present: 6,000 − 780 workers remaining = 5,220 workers displaced/6,000 = 87 percent displacement rate, or 7,000 − 780 = 6,220/7,000 = 88.9 percent displacement rate.

Notes

1 Agriculture and the comparative analysis of production systems

1 For an analysis of the effects of Stalinism on Marxian movements in Western Europe, see Anderson 1976. Although not dealing with the United States, most of Anderson's analysis is directly applicable. Parenthetically, it should be noted that Marxist scholars did not completely ignore agriculture although much of their analysis was concerned with either the transition to capitalism (Kautsky 1899; Lenin 1943a,b) or explanations, following Mao Tse-tung's essays (1967a,b) on class structure and the successes of the peasant-based Chinese revolution, about the revolutionary character of peasants. More recently, a number of Francophonic Marxists working in Africa and the Third World have returned to agricultural analysis.

2 Few systematic attempts have been made to integrate the empirical materials and theoretical concepts of industrial sociology with labor process analysis. Burawoy (1979, 14–16) has made major strides in this direction with his distinction between relations-of-production and relations-in-production. Clearly, more critical assessment of prior work in industrial sociology will yield important insights for understanding change in capitalist production systems.

3 Among the most important land grant universities in this respect are those of California, Wisconsin, Michigan, Illinois, Iowa, and Cornell University.

4 This is not to contend that places in which there are relatively low population densities no longer exist. There are still many; but the way of life that characterizes most people and communities of low density, despite the assiduous claims of the USDA about the turnaround in population movement, is *urban* and not rural. Just because suburbs spread farther away from cities or more people have two homes does not mean that rural society exists. Equally, just because there are some isolated and genuinely rural communities in a few geographical backwaters does not prove the continued viability of rural life. It is time for U.S. sociology and rural sociology to face the fact that rurality as a social phenomenon has essentially disappeared in the United States.

5 However, in constructing our projections in Chapter 4 on the effects of harvest mechanization, we necessarily broaden our focus to encompass community-based changes.

6 Cf., Friedland (1979) for further discussion of the emphasis in rural sociology on community, rather than on class and production issues. There are a few, too few, exceptions to this, notably the work of Rodefeld (1974) and T. Lynn Smith (1969).

7 For a general discussion of farm organizations see McCune 1956; for a discussion of California farm organization see Chambers 1952.

8 In grapes, for example, the various commodity associations in California include the Desert Grape Advisory Board (a state marketing order [MO]), the California Table Grape Commission, the Raisin Administrative Commission (a federal MO), the California Raisin Advisory Board (MO), the Raisin Bargaining Association, Sun-Maid (a

144

production and marketing co-op), the Wine Institute (an association of wine producers), the Wine Advisory Board (defunct as an MO since 1975), the California Association of Winegrape Growers (an attempt to create a wine grape growers bargaining association), as well as about half a dozen regional associations of wine grape growers. There is also the American Society of Enologists, a national professional association largely based in California. The California Table Grape Commission, it should be noted, although functioning very much like a marketing order organization, was created through a special act of the California State Legislature rather than through marketing order legislation. Effectively, this means that the commission does not have to report to the Department of Food and Agriculture and has no effective supervising administrative agency.

9 For a more detailed discussion of this process see Fellmeth 1971; Fiske 1979, Chapter 4; Friedland and Kappel 1979; Galarza 1977; Kappel 1979; McConnell 1969.

2 Theory and method

1 The term *bracero* refers to Mexican nationals recruited under an international agreement between the U.S. and Mexican governments that operated between 1942 and 1964. Although the program went through various revisions during its twenty-two-year span, the basic practices involved remained the same throughout its lifetime. Braceros (those who work with their hands) were recruited from interior villages of Mexico based on projected demands for labor in the United States. These demands were translated into labor certifications passed from U.S. government officials to Mexican labor recruiters. For more historical details about the bracero program see Galarza 1964, Craig 1971, and Hancock 1959.

2 See, for example, Fuller and Van Vuuren 1972; Fuller and Mason 1977; Fuller and Mamer 1978.

3 See, for example, Taylor 1930, 1937, 1938a,b; Taylor and Vasey 1936a,b.

4 Two notable exceptions will be found in the dissertations of Smith (1961) and Glass (1966). The first, although concerned with lettuce production as an overall system, develops the analysis of technology and labor; the Glass dissertation is especially valuable in demonstrating the connection between technology, the labor process, and the state of union organization.

5 Projective methodology, it should be noted, fits into that developing area of research known as Social Impact Assessment (cf., Wolf 1976; Finsterbusch and Wolf 1977). Also, in formulating the approach used here, we are drawing on a considerable literature that has been concerned with the analysis of existing social trends.

6 The section is based on an earlier study, *Destalking The Wily Tomato,* Friedland and Barton (1975), also presented in summary form in Friedland and Barton (1976). A study by Scheuring and Thompson (1978) provides material on tomato harvesting following the introduction of the electronic sorter. We have also drawn on this study in this section. Processing tomatoes are used for canning and freezing and in soups, sauces, ketchup, as well as in many other processed foods. In this study, when we refer to tomatoes we will be discussing only processing tomatoes and not tomatoes intended for the fresh market, unless specifically designated fresh market tomatoes.

3 The social organization of lettuce production

1 Some of the publications indicating the character of research in lettuce over the decades can be seen by examining Zahara, et al. 1960; Zahara and McCoy 1963; Burns and

Podany 1973; Ceponis and Griffin 1963; Englund and Jones 1966; Foytik 1972; Kader et al. 1973; Lipton et al. 1972; Wellman 1926; Whitaker et al. 1974; and other articles and monographs cited in the bibliography. This inventory constitutes only a small segment of the relevant materials available.

2 We are especially grateful to Hub Segur for sharing with us his considerable knowledge developed through his own study of the lettuce production system.

3 Data have been derived from annual reports of the Federal State Market News Service (MNS). See *Marketing Lettuce–Marketing Season*, annual reports for the Salinas and Imperial districts. Undoubtedly, some lettuce movement escapes the attentions of the MNS. The MNS is, however, very active in assembling data from shipping points; although some localized production from farmer to local markets may occur, the bulk of commercial lettuce is carefully scrutinized by the MNS and the data reported are probably among the most accurate available in the entire lettuce production system.

4 Although California and Arizona constitute a single production area, the data reported in Table 3.3 are based on California alone. The data are the product of a study conducted through a marketing order limited to California production. Similarly, the categories reported on are "handlers" rather than grower-shippers. Because some "handlers" may be firms that do not grow and/or ship lettuce but are brokers or sales agents, the data reported must be treated with some care.

5 There is one major exception to the discussion that follows. Employees of Bud Antle have been under contract with the Teamsters Union since 1961 and these workers can be considered to have been semi-internalized or internalized since that time.

6 This subject is being researched by one of the authors and will constitute a more thorough sociological analysis, see Thomas 1980c.

7 Research has been conducted by one of the authors; see Thomas 1978, 1980c.

8 In this report we will utilize EDD to refer to the present agency and all its antecedent organizations. When referring to a publication, reference will be made to the name of the specific agency publishing the report.

9 The use of organization as a weapon is notable in American agriculture although the concept itself originates in other circumstances (Selznick 1952). By organization weapon we mean the capacity to organize a group and utilize the organization for distinctive purposes. In U.S. agriculture this capacity has been noted, although without utilization of the specific concept of organization as weapon, by many writers. See, for example, McConnell 1969, Selznick 1953, McCune 1956; for California, see Chambers 1952, Galarza 1977: pp. 47–55.

10 In 1978 a change in the managerial organization of Inter Harvest also resulted in a change in the name of the organization to Sun Harvest. We will use the names Inter Harvest and Sun Harvest interchangeably according to the time being referred to. Ownership by United Brands remained intact during this change.

11 Although no data are available on Sun Harvest, there is some agreement in the industry that this firm is one of the largest of the grower-shippers. The Antle firm prides itself on its size, which can be seen in Table 3.9. Data on Bruce Church have been provided by an article in *The Grower*, a regular publication issued by *The Packer* (see Linden 1977b). Some data on Finerman were provided in an advertising supplement to the *Packer*, Dec. 21, 1974.

12 Thus Jerry Goldstine was senior vice-president of the Finerman organization. "Goldstine's father and Finerman's father were . . . business partners in a wholesaling firm in Chicago," (Finerman 1974, p. 14C). Bud Antle began working around agriculture in the 1930s; he later developed his organization and, despite ups and downs, emerged as the

largest single lettuce producer prior to the creation of Inter Harvest. Other lettuce firms such as Merrill, Garin, Englund, and the like also began as buying or selling agents who developed into sizable firms during the 1930s and 1940s.

13 See the Antle company's promotional brochure, "Where the People Make the Difference."

14 For additional detail on the Antle organization see Fredricks 1978; 1979. Further data are available on Antle through a stock prospectus prepared by the company in 1972 when the company intended to "go public." For some reason unknown to the writers, the company never went public. Reference to the stock prospectus will be to Antle 1972 here.

15 Space does not permit provision of details on this complex battle, suffice it to note that, after years of litigation, a court suit forced the Interior Department to agree to enforce the limitation on land ownership to which water has been provided through federal subsidies. The Citizens for Government Fairness organization is especially interesting because it constitutes a distinctive organization through which Imperial Valley farmers have separated themselves from growers elsewhere in California and the West who have benefited through federal water policies. Imperial growers, like other western growers, prefer to have no limitations on acreages but are hedging their bets with respect to their own situation by organizational separation, basing themselves on the historic differences in the origins of water for irrigation in the Imperial Valley.

16 In the Salinas Valley the Farm Bureau effort was focused on the Salinas Valley Independent Growers Association (SVIGA). SVIGA provides its members with labor relations advice and insurance services for employees of its member-subscribers. The relationship of lettuce grower-shippers to SVIGA is not clear; we believe SVIGA's membership is drawn from growers in the Salinas Valley including lettuce growers who grow the crop for grower-shipper firms rather than from the growing-shipping firms.

17 California's interests with respect to coverage of agricultural workers under the National Labor Relations Act are distinctively different from those of Arizona, which has an act that is favorable to growers, and Florida, Texas, or Oregon, which have no such legislation. The WGA favors NLRA coverage, whereas grower organizations and growers elsewhere are less favorable or opposed to the NLRA coverage (*Packer*, 1977b).

18 Research involving lettuce, which can be important if there is a shift to mechanized harvesting, is voluminous. See, for example, Stout et al. 1973; Cargill and Garrett 1975; Hinsch and Rij 1976; Rij et al. 1976.

19 Considerable research has been devoted to the development of the "square" tomato, a tomato whose shape is much boxier than the traditional round one. The square tomato has been bred for machine harvesting because it is less subject to rolling and bruising than round tomatoes.

20 The following section is based on Windslow 1976a,b; Razee 1976.

21 In January 1978, Roger Garrett for the Davis group and Don Lenker for the Salinas group, announced that development would now stop, apparently as a result of grower-shipper lack of interest in adoption. Several additional commercial prototypes have been developed by private firms and are being tested on a small scale. Little public information is available on these prototypes.

22 On postharvest handling see Stout et al. 1973; Cargill and Garrett 1975; Hinsch et al. 1976; Hinsch and Rij 1976; Rij et al. 1976; Johnson and Zahara 1976b; *Western Grower and Shipper*, December 1977, pp. 11–12; interviews with Paul Adrian and Roger Garrett.

23 In this respect, lettuce harvesting research has benefited from prior research in processing tomatoes where the handling problem was not grappled with until after the cutting and selection problems were resolved (Friedland and Barton 1975, p. 25).

4 Projected consequences of technological change in the lettuce industry

1 A later article by Leeper (1980) points out that "the New York City consumer is paying 15 cents just for the delivery of each head of California lettuce." The increased cost is a reflection of the sharp increase in petroleum fuels for truck transport, the predominant means of shipping lettuce.

2 Master Agreement between Inter Harvest, Inc., and the United Farm Workers, AFL-CIO, Article 6, p.17.

3 600 cartons × 10 hours per day = 6,000 cartons = 6 carlots; 6 carlots × 300 days = 1,800 carlots. Readers may note some discrepancies in the harvester capacity. Adrian reports machine potential at 450–700 cartons/hour although in the prototype tests a capacity of 400 cartons was reported. Johnson and Zahara (1976b) use a capacity of 480 cartons/hour in their calculations. We will use these various figures in constructing our projections.

4 See Miklius and DeLoach 1965; Foytik 1972; Garoyan 1974; Federal Trade Commission 1976: Vol. 83, 1614–715; *Federal Supplement*, 1976: "Northern California Supermarkets vs. Central California Lettuce Producers Cooperative," Vol. 413, 984–94.

5 In the UFW–Sun Harvest contract of 1979 (p.71) closers are paid $5.45 per hour and packers receive $5.30; cutters and wrappers, on the other hand, are paid $5.10 per hour.

6 In 1970 the population of Mexicali was 396,324. See Gobierno del Estado de Baja California Norte 1977, Table 1.0.

5 Conclusion

1 For a more advanced discussion of asymmetric power relations among firms in the same industry and a typology of those relations see Soule 1979.

Bibliography

Agricultural Research. 1974. "Harvesting Lettuce Electronically." Washington, D.C.: U.S. Dept. of Agriculture. January, pp. 8–11.

Aldrich, Howard E. 1979. *Organization and Environments.* Englewood Cliffs, N.J.: Prentice-Hall.

Allen, Rutillus H. 1934. *Economic History of Agriculture in Monterey County, California During the American Period.* Ph.D. dissertation, University of California, Berkeley, Dept. of Agricultural Economics.

Anderson, Perry. 1976. *Considerations in Western Marxism.* London: New Left Books.

Antle, Bud. 1972. "Bud of California: 550,000 Shares, Bud Antle, Inc." Preliminary Prospectus dated May 11.

Beale, Calvin. 1978. "People on the Land." In Thomas R. Ford (ed.), *Rural U.S.A.: Persistence and Change.* Ames: Iowa State University Press: Chapter 3, pp. 37–54.

Bernstein, Irving. 1970. *The Turbulent Years.* Boston: Houghton Mifflin.

Blauner, Robert. 1964. *Alienation and Freedom.* Chicago: University of Chicago Press.

Braverman, Harry. 1974. *Labor and Monopoly Capital: The Degradation of Work in the Twentieth Century.* New York: Monthly Review Press.

Brewster, John M. 1950. "The Machine Process in Agriculture and Industry." *Journal of Farm Economics, 32,* 1:69–81.

Bricker, Jack. 1976. "Field-Level Palletizing Program Cuts Damage to Wrapped Lettuce," *The Packer,* July 31.

Burawoy, Michael. 1979. *Manufacturing Consent: Changes in the Labor Process Under Monopoly Capitalism.* Chicago: University of Chicago Press.

Burns, Alfred J. and Joseph C. Podany. 1973. *Lettuce Prices, Costs and Margins.* Washington, D.C.: U.S. Dept. of Agriculture, The Vegetable Situation, No. 190.

California Iceberg Lettuce Research Program. 1976. *Annual Report.* Sacramento: CILRP. 1977. *Annual Report.* Sacramento: CILRP.

Cargill, B. F. and R. E. Garrett. 1975. "The 'Big Picture' of Lettuce Handling." *Transactions of the American Society of Agricultural Engineers, 18:* 7–9.

Ceponis, M. J. and G. J. Griffin. 1963. *Effects of Heat-Tunnel Temperatures on the Quality of Shrink-Film-Wrapped Lettuce.* Washington, D.C.: U.S. Dept. of Agriculture, Marketing Research Report No. 634.

Chambers, Clarke A. 1952. *California Farm Organizations.* Berkeley: University of California Press.

Chandler, Alfred D. Jr. 1969. *Strategy and Structure: Chapters in the History of the American Industrial Enterprise.* Cambridge, Mass.: M.I.T. Press.

Conrad, David E. 1965. *The Forgotten Farmers.* Urbana: University of Illinois.

Craig, Richard. 1971. *The Bracero Program.* Austin: University of Texas Press.

Dahl, Robert A. 1971. *Who Governs?* New Haven: Yale University Press.

Doeringer, Peter B. and Michael J. Piore. 1971. *Internal Labor Markets and Manpower Analysis.* Lexington, Mass.: Health.

Drossler Associates. 1976. "Results of the Distribution Research Study Conducted for the California Iceberg Lettuce Advisory Board." San Francisco.

Englund, Walter J. and Kenneth R. Jones. 1966. *Condition and Outlook Report for the California Head Lettuce Industry.* Sacramento: California Dept. of Agriculture, Bureau of Marketing.

Enochian, R. V., F. J. Smith, and L. L. Sammet. 1955. *Costs and Efficiency in Field Packing Western Head Lettuce.* Davis: California Agricultural Experiment Station, Giannini Foundation of Agricultural Economics, Report No. 183. 1957. *Cost and Efficiency in House Packing Western Head Lettuce.* Davis: California Agricultural Experiment Station, Giannini Foundation of Agricultural Economics. Report No. 199.

Federal-State Market News Service. 1976. *Marketing Lettuce from the Salinas-Watsonville-King City and Other Central California Districts.* Sacramento: Department of Food and Agriculture, Division of Marketing Services, Annual Report.

Federal Supplement. 1976. *Volume 413,* pp. 984–94.

Federal Trade Commission. 1976. "In The Matter of United Brands Company." *Decisions: Findings, Opinions, and Orders, 83:* 1614–76. Washington, D.C.: U.S. Government Printing Office. 1977. "In the Matter of Central California Lettuce Producers Cooperative, et al." *Decisions: Findings, Opinions, and Orders, 90:* 18–63. Washington, D.C.: U.S. Government Printing Office.

Fellmeth, Robert C. 1971. *Power and Land in California.* Washington D.C.: Center for Study of Responsive Law.

Finerman, Mel. 1974. *Mel Finerman Co., Inc.,* Advertising Supplement to *The Packer,* December 21.

Finsterbusch, Kurt and C. P. Wolf (eds.). 1977. *Methods of Social Impact Assessment.* Stroudsburg, Penn.: Dowden, Hutchinson, and Ross.

Firch, Robert S. and Daniel W. Mathews. (nd) *The Arizona Lettuce Industry.* University of Arizona.

Fisher, Lloyd H. 1953. *The Harvest Labor Market in California.* Cambridge, Mass.: Harvard University Press.

Fiske, Emmett. 1979. *The College and the Constituency: Rural and Community Development at the University of California 1875–1978.* Ph.D. dissertation, Davis: University of California. Ann Arbor: University Microfilms, 1980.

Fortune. 1977. "The Fortune Directory of the 500 Largest U.S. Industrial Corporations." May.

Foytik, Jerry. 1955. *California Lettuce Marketing Channels and Farm to Retail Margins.* Davis: California Agricultural Experiment Station, Giannini Foundation of Agricultural Economics. Report No. 182. 1972. "Competition in the Lettuce Industry." Davis: University of California, Dept. of Agricultural Economics. Statement to F.T.C. hearing, July.

Franta, Harry. 1975. "Antle Enters Pre-Cut Lettuce Business," *The Packer,* October 18, p.1,6.

Fredricks, Anne. 1978. *California Agribusiness: A Case Study.* Senior thesis, Community Studies, University of California, Santa Cruz. 1979. "Agribusiness in the Lettuce Fields." *Food Monitor,* No. 10, May–June:12–15.

Friedland, William H. 1967. "Migrant Labor: A Form of Intermittent Social Organization." *ILR Research, 13,* 2, November 3–14. Also published in Subcommittee on Migratory Labor and Public Welfare, U.S. Senate, 90th Congress, Second Session, *Hearings on*

Migratory Labor Legislation, part 4, Appendix II: 965–1003. 1974. *Social Sleepwalkers: Scientific and Technological Research in California Agriculture.* Davis: University of California, Dept. of Applied Behavioral Sciences. Research Monograph No. 13. 1978. "Social Influences on the Production of Knowledge." Paper read to the Fulbright–Hays Western Regional Conference. 1979. "Who Killed Rural Sociology? A Case Study in the Political Economy of Knowledge Production." Paper read at the 1979 meeting of The American Sociological Association.

Friedland, William H. and Amy Barton. 1975. *Destalking the Wily Tomato: A Case Study in Social Consequences in California Agricultural Research.* Davis: University of California, Dept. of Applied Behavioral Sciences. Research Monograph No. 15. 1976. "Tomato Technology." *Society, 13,* 6, September/October:34–42.

Friedland, William H. and Tim Kappel. 1979. *Production of Perish: Changing the Inequities of Agricultural Research Priorities.* Santa Cruz: University of California, Project on Social Impact Assessment and Values.

Friedland, William H. and Dorothy Nelkin. 1972. "Technological Trends and the Organization of Migrant Farm Workers." *Social Problems, 19,* 4, Spring:509–21.

Friedland, William H. and Robert J. Thomas. 1974. "Paradoxes of Agricultural Unionism in California." *Society, 11,* 4, May/June:54–62.

Fuller, Varden and John W. Mamer. 1978. "Constraints on California Farm Worker Organization." *Industrial Relations, 17,* 2:143–55.

Fuller, Varden and Bert Mason. 1977. "Farm Labor," *Annals of the American Academy of Political and Social Science, 429:*63–80.

Fuller, Varden and William Van Vuuren. 1972. "Farm Labor and Labor Markets." In A. Gordon Ball and Earl O. Heady (eds.), *Size, Structure, and Future of Farms.* Ames: Iowa State University Press. Chapter 9,pp.144–70.

Galarza, Ernesto. 1964. *Merchants of Labor: The Mexican Bracero Story.* Charlotte, N.C.: McNally and Loftin. 1977. *Farm Workers and Agri-business in California, 1947-1960.* Notre Dame: University of Notre Dame Press.

Garoyan, Leon. 1974. "Some Economic Considerations of the California Iceberg Lettuce Industry." Unpublished paper, University of California, Davis, Dept. of Agricultural Economics.

Garrett, R. E., M. Zahara and R. E. Griffin. 1966. "Selector-Component Development for a Head-Lettuce Harvester." *Transactions of the American Society of Agricultural Engineers, 9,*1:56–7.

Glass, Judith Chanin. 1966. *Conditions Which Facilitate Unionization of Agricultural Workers: A Case Study of the Salinas Valley Lettuce Industry.* Ph. D. dissertation, University of California, Los Angeles, Dept. of Economics.

Gobierno Del Estado de Baja California Norte. 1977. *Datos Estadisticos.* Comite Promotor del Desarrollo Socioeconomico.

Goldschmidt, Walter. 1978. *As You Sow: Three Studies in the Social Consequences of Agribusiness.* Montclair, N.J.: Allanheld, Osmun.

Gourlie, John. 1963. "Raising Lettuce 10 Months a Year." *Organic Gardening and Farming,* June:18–21.

Hagar, Dan. 1977. "First Michigan Lettuce Shredder Bargaining for Midwest Market." *The Packer,* September 3.

Hancock, Richard. 1959. *The Role of the Bracero Program on the Economic and Cultural Dynamics of Mexico.* Stanford, Calif.: Hispanic–American Society.

Harriott, B. L. and K. K. Barnes. 1964. "Mechanical Selection of Crisphead Lettuce for Harvest." *Transactions of the ASAE, 7,* 3:195–96,199.

Harriott, B. L., K. K. Barnes, E. O. Finch, and P. M. Bessey. 1964. "Mechanical Harvest of Crisphead Lettuce." *Agricultural Engineering*, November.

Hathaway, Dale E. 1972. "The State of Social Science Research in the United States Department of Agriculture and the State Agricultural Experiment Stations." Appendix P:400–31. In *National Research Council, Report of the Committee on Research Advisory* to the U.S. Dept. of Agriculture, Appendices b-r, National Technical Information Service.

Heelan, Patrick A. 1975. "Werner Karl Heisenberg." *Encyclopedia Britannica, 8:*745–6. Chicago: Encyclopedia Britannica.

Hinsch, R. Tom and Roger E. Rij. 1976. *Packing and Shipping Mechanically Harvested Lettuce*. Washington, D.C.: U.S. Dept. of Agriculture. Marketing Research Report No. 1049.

Hinsch, R. Tom, Roger E. Rij, and Joseph K. Stewart. 1976. *Quality of Iceberg Lettuce in Film Overwraps During Simulated Export*. Washington, D.C.: U.S. Dept. of Agriculture, Agriculture Research Service.

Hoos, Sidney and Fisk H. Phelps. 1958. *Commercial Head Lettuce, Economic Status, 1947*. Berkeley: University of California, The College of Agriculture. California Agricultural Experiment Station Circular 378, February.

Jamieson, Stuart. 1945. *Labor Unionism in American Agriculture*. Washington D.C.: U.S. Government Printing Office.

Johnson, Stanley S. and Mike Zahara. 1976a. *Lettuce Harvesting and Packing: Hand and Machine Harvest Alternatives*. Washington, D.C.: U.S. Dept. of Agriculture. The Vegetable Situation 200. 1976b. "Prospective Lettuce Harvest Mechanization: Impact on Labor." *Journal of the American Society for Horticultural Science, 101,* 4:378–81.

Jones, H. A. and A. A. Tavernetti. 1932. *The Head-Lettuce Industry of California*. Berkeley: University of California, California Agricultural Extension Service. Circular 60.

Jones, William O. 1947. *The Salinas Valley: Its Agricultural Development, 1920–40* Ph.D. dissertation, Stanford University, Dept. of Economics.

Kader, Adel A., Werner J. Lipton, and Leonard L. Morris. 1973. "Systems for Scoring Quality of Harvested Lettuce." *Hort Science 8, 5,* October:408–9.

Kappel, Tim. 1979. *Fermentation Without Representation: Structural Influences on the Setting of Priorities for Publicly-Funded Wine Research*. Santa Cruz: University of California, Board of Community Studies. Senior Thesis.

Kautsky, Karl. 1899. *Die Agrarfrage*. Stuttgart: Dietz.

Kelly, C. F. 1966. "Preface" in *Research on Agricultural Mechanization*. Agricultural Experiment Station, University of California.

Kendrick, J. B., Jr. 1977. "Social Impact of Agricultural Research." *California Agriculture, 31,* 6, June:2.

Kraft, Philip. 1977. *Programmers and Managers: The Routinization of Computer Programmers in the United States*. New York: Springer-Verlag.

Lamb, Helen B. 1942. *Industrial Relations in the Western Lettuce Industry*. Ph.D. dissertation, Radcliffe College, Dept. of History, Government and Economics.

Landsberger, Henry. 1958. *Hawthorne Revisited: Management and the Worker: Its Critics and Developments in Human Relations in Industry*. Ithaca: N.Y. State School of Industrial and Labor Relations.

Lappé, Frances Moore, Joseph Collins, with Cary Fowler. 1979. *Food First: Beyond the Myth of Scarcity*. New York: Ballantine.

Leeper, Donald S. 1980. "Lettuce: 1. Food, 2. Money, 3. Energy." *New York Times,* May 14.

Lenin, V. I. 1943a. "The Agrarian Question in Russia at the End of the Nineteenth Century." In *Selected Works, Vol.1.* New York: International Publishers, pp.13–91. 1943b. "The Development of Capitalism in Russia." In *Selected Works, Vol. 1.* New York: International Publishers, pp.95–259.

Lenker, D. H., P. A. Adrian, G. W. French, and Mike Zahara. 1973. "Selective Mechanical Lettuce Harvesting System." *Transactions of the American Society of Agricultural Engineers, 16,* 5:858–61, 866.

Lerner, William (ed.). 1975. *Historical Statistics of the United States: Colonial Times to 1970.* Part I. Washington, D.C.:U.S. Government Printing Office.

Lewin, Kurt. 1951. *Field Theory in the Social Sciences.* New York: Harper and Row.

Linden, Tim. 1977a. "Smith Trims Head, Handling: His Processors Never Had It So Good." *The Packer,* July 30. 1977b. "Putting the Wraps on the Lettuce Industry." *The Grower.* In *The Packer,* August:6b–7b.

Lipset, Seymour Martin, Martin A. Trow, and James S. Coleman. 1956. *Union Democracy.* Glencoe, Ill.: Free Press.

Lipton, W. J., J. K. Stewart, and T. W. Whitaker. 1972. *An Illustrated Guide to the Identification of Some Market Disorders of Head Lettuce.* Wahington, D.C.: U.S. Dept. of Agriculture. Marketing Research Report No. 950.

Mackintosh, Maureen. 1977. "Fruit and Vegetables as an International Commodity: The Relocation of Horticultural Production and Its Implications for the Producers." *Food Policy,* Novenber, 277–92.

Malinowski, Bronislaw. 1948. *Magic, Science, and Religion.* Garden City, N.Y.: Doubleday.

Mandel, Ernest. 1975. *Late Capitalism.* London: New Left Books.

Manning, Helen. 1977. "Man Outworks Lettuce Machine," *Salinas Californian,* August 25.

Mao Tse-tung. 1967a. "Analysis of the Classes in Chinese Society." In *Selected Works, Vol. 1.* Peking: Foreign Language Press., pp.13–21. 1967b. "Report of an Investigation of the Peasant Movement in Hunan." In *Selected Works, Vol. 1.* Peking: Foreign Language Press., pp.23–59.

Marglin, Stephen. 1974. "What Do Bosses Do?" *Review of Radical Political Economy, 6, 2,* Summer: 60–122.

Mayo, Elton. 1945. *The Social Problems of an Industrial Civilization.* Boston: Harvard University, Graduate School of Business Administration.

McCann, Thomas P. 1976. *An American Company: The Tragedy of United Fruit.* New York: Crown.

McConnell, Grant. 1969. *The Decline of Agrarian Democracy.* New York: Atheneum.

McCune, Wesley. 1956. *Who's Behind Our Farm Policy?* New York: Praeger.

McWilliams, Carey. 1971. *Factories in the Field.* Santa Barbara: Peregrine.

Merton, Robert K. 1936. "The Unanticipated Consequences of Purposive Social Action." *American Sociological Review, 1, 6,* December:894–904.

Miklius, Walter. 1967. "Estimating the Demand for Truck and Rail Transportation: A Case Study of California Lettuce." *Agricultural Economics Research, 19, 2,* April:46–50.

Miklius, Walter and D. B. DeLoach. 1965. "Do Lettuce Buyers Exert Oligopsony Power?" *Agricultural Economics Research,* October:101–7.

Miliband, Ralph. 1969. *The State in Capitalist Society.* New York: Basic Books.

Miller, David C. 1977. "Methods of Estimating Societal Futures." In Kurt Finsterbusch and C. P. Wolf (eds.), *Methodology of Social Impact Assessment.* Stroudsburg, Penn.: Dowden, Hutchinson and Ross:202–10.

Mills, C. Wright. 1951. *White Collar.* New York: Oxford University Press.

154   *Bibliography*

Moore, C. V. and Herbert J. Snyder. 1969. *Risk and Uncertainity in Lettuce Production in Salinas Valley,* California. Davis: California Agricultural Experiment Station, Giannini Foundation of Agriculture Economics. Report No. 300.

Moore, Wilbert. 1951. *Industrial Relations and the Social Order.* New York: Macmillan.

Morin, Alexander. 1952. *The Organization of Farm Labor in the United States.* Cambridge, Mass.: Harvard University Press. Harvard Studies in Labor in Agriculture, No. 2-HL.

Noble, David. 1978. "Social Choice in Machine Design: The Case of Automatically Controlled Machine Tools, and a Challenge for Labor." *Politics and Society, 8,* 3–4:313–47.

Nolan, Michael F., Robert A. Hagen, and Mary S. Hoekstra. 1975. "Rural Sociological Research, 1966–1974: Implications for Social Policy." *Rural Sociology, 40,* 4:435–54.

The Packer. 1975. " 'No' to California Lettuce Order." *The Packer,* December 13. 1977a. *The Packer's Produce Availability & Merchandising Guide.* Kansas City, Kansas: Vance Publishing. 1977b. "Panel Looks at Farm Labor Issues." *The Packer,* May 21.

Padfield, Harland and William E. Martin. 1965. *Farmers, Workers and Machines: Technological and Social Change in Farm Industries of Arizona.* Tucson: University of Arizona Press.

Paige, Jeffery M. 1975. *Agrarian Revolution.* New York: Free Press.

Perrow, Charles. 1968. "The Effect of Technological Change on the Structure of Business Firms." In B. C. Roberts (ed.), *Industrial Relations: Contemporary Issues.* New York: St. Martin's Press:205–19.

Rasmussen, Wayne D. 1960. *Findings in the History of American Agriculture.* Urbana: University of Illinois Press. 1968. "Advances in American Agriculture: The Mechanized Tomato Harvester as a Case Study." *Technology and Culture, 9:*531–43.

Razee, Don. 1976. "The Advantages of Transplanting Lettuce." *California Farmer,* November 20:6. 1981. "Scarred Veteran's Non-Unionization Tips." *California Farmer,* February 2:30–1.

Rij, Roger E., Russel H. Hinds, and Tom R. Hinsch. 1976. *Current Practices and Trends in Marketing Western Iceberg Lettuce in Relation to Other Produce.* Washington, D.C.: U.S. Dept. of Agriculture, Marketing Research Report No. 1052.

Rodefeld, Richard D. 1974. *The Changing Organizational and Occupational Structure of Farming and the Implications for Farm Workforce Individuals, Families, and Communities.* Ph.D. dissertation, University of Wisconsin.

Roethlissberger, F. J. and William J. Dickson. 1939. *Management and the Worker.* Cambridge, Mass.: Harvard University Press.

Rogers, Everett M. 1962. *Diffusion of Innovations.* Glencoe, Ill.: Free Press.

Scheuring, Ann F. and O. E. Thompson. 1978. *From Lug Boxes to Electronics: A Study of California Tomato Growers and Sorting Crews.* Davis: University of California, California Agricultural Policy Seminar, Monograph No. 3.

Schnaiberg, Allan and Errol Meidinger. 1978. "Social Reality Versus Analytic Mythology: Social Impact Assessment of Natural Resource Utilization." Paper read at the 1978 meeting of the American Sociological Association.

Selznick, Philip. 1952. *The Organizational Weapon.* New York: McGraw-Hill. 1953. *TVA and the Grass roots.* Berkeley: University of California Press.

Shepardson, E. S., J. G. Pollock, and G. E. Rehkugler. 1973. "Mechanical Harvester for New York Lettuce." *New York's Food and Life Sciences, 6 2,* April–June:13–15.

Sheppard, Harold. 1949. "The Treatment of Unionism in 'Managerial Sociology.'" *American Sociological Review, 14:*310–13. 1950. "The Social and Historical Philosophy of Elton Mayo." *Antioch Review, 10:*396–406.

Smith, Frank. 1961. *The Impact of Technological Change in the Marketing of Salinas Lettuce.* Ph.D. dissertation, Berkeley: University of California.

Smith, Frank J., L. L. Sammet, and Robert V. Enochian. 1955. *Costs and Efficiency in Field Packing Western Head Lettuce.* University of California, Experimental Station, Giannini Foundation, Mimeographed Report No. 183.

Smith, T. Lynn. 1969. "A Study of Social Stratification on the Agricultural Sections of the U.S.: Nature, Data, Procedures, and Preliminary Results." *Rural Sociology, 34,* 4:496–509.

Soule, W. T. 1979. "Inequality Among Organizations and the Historical Construction of Industries." Unpublished paper, Department of Sociology, Northwestern University.

Stinchcombe, Arthur. 1959. "Bureaucratic and Craft Administration of Production: A Comparative Study." *Administrative Science Quarterly, 4:*168–87. 1961. "Agricultural Enterprise and Rural Class Relations." *American Journal of Sociology,* 67:165–76.

Stokes, C. Shannon and Michael K. Miller. 1975. "A Methodological Review of Research in *Rural Sociology* Since 1965." *Rural Sociology, 40,* 4, Winter:411–19.

Stout, B. A., R. F. Kasmire, and V. E. Rubatzky. 1973. "Bulk Bin Handling of Crisphead Lettuce." *Transactions of the American Society of Agricultural Engineers,* January–February:62–63.

Street, James H. 1957. *The New Revolution in the Cotton Economy: Mechanization and its Consequences.* Chapel Hill: The University of North Carolina.

Taylor, Carl C. 1952. *The Farmer's Movement, 1620–1920.* New York: American Book Co.

Taylor, Paul S. 1930. *Mexican Labor in the United States.* Berkeley: University of California Press. 1937. "Migratory Farm Labor in the United States." *Monthly Labor Review, 44,* 3, March:537–49. 1938a. "Power Farming and Labor Displacement in the Cotton Belt." *Monthly Labor Review, 46,* 3, March:595–607. 1938b. "Power Farming and Labor Displacement." Part 2, *Monthly Labor Review, 46,* 4, April:852–67.

Taylor, Paul S. and Clark Kerr. 1940. "Documentary History of the Strike of Cotton Pickers in California, 1933." Hearings before a Subcommittee of the Committee on Education and Labor, U.S. Senate, 76th Congress, Third Session (the LaFollete Hearings).

Taylor, Paul S. and Tom Vasey. 1936a. "Historical Background of California Farm Labor," *Rural Sociology, 1,* 3, September:281–95. 1936b. "Contemporary Background of California Farm Labor." *Rural Sociology, 1,* 4, December:401–19.

Thomas, Robert J. 1978. "Systems of Labor Control in Industrial Agriculture." Unpublished paper, Department of Sociology, Northwestern University. 1980a. "Framework for the Study of Agricultural Industrialization." Paper presented at the annual meeting of the Midwest Sociological Association, April. 1980b. "The Social Organization of Industrial Agriculture." Paper presented at the annual meeting of the American Sociological Association, August. 1980c. *Citizenship and Labor Supply: The Social Organization of Industrial Agriculture.* Ph.D. Dissertation, Evanston, Ill.: Department of Sociology, Northwestern University.

Thompson, James D. 1967. *Organizations in Action.* New York: McGraw-Hill.

U.S. Department of Labor. 1966. *Technological Trends in Major American Industries.* Bulletin No. 1474. Washington, D.C.: U.S. Government Printing Office.

U.S. Senate. 1941. *Violations of Free Speech and Rights of Labor.* Hearings before a Subcommittee of the Committee of Education and Labor, 76th Congress, Third Session. Part 73. Washington, D.C.: U.S. Government Printing Office. 1975. "Marketing Lettuce in the United States." In Economic Research Service, U.S. Dept. of Agricul-

156   *Bibliography*

ture, *The Market Function and Costs For Food Between American's Fields and Tables.* Prepared for the Subcommittee on Agricultural Production, Marketing and Stabilization of Prices, Committee on Agriculture and Forestry, U.S. Senate, March 25 by the Economic Research Service and Agriculture Marketing Service, U.S. Dept. of Agriculture.

The Vegetable Situation. 1973. *Lettuce Prices, Costs and Margins.* Washington, D.C.: U.S. Dept. of Agriculture.

Vlachos, Evan. 1977. "The Use of Scenarios for Social Impact Assessment." In Kurt Finsterbusch and C. P. Wolf (eds.), *Methodology of Social Impact Assessment.* Stroudsburg, Penn.: Dowden, Hutchinson, and Ross, pp.211–223.

Waterfield, Larry. 1976. "Researchers Breed Lettuce for Florida," *The Packer,* December 4:11a.

Watson, Don. 1977. "Rise and Decline of Fruit Tramp Unionism in the Western Lettuce Industry." Paper prepared for the Southwest Labor Studies Conference, Tempe, Arizona, March 4.

Wellman, H. R. 1926. *Series on California Crops and Prices: Lettuce.* Berkeley: University of California, California Agricultural Extension Service, Circular 5.

Western Growers and Shippers Association. 1973. "Lettuce Harvester Gets Mechanical Trimmer." *Western Grower and Shipper,* January:5–6,8.

Whitaker, T. W., E. J. Ryder, V. E. Rubatsky, and P. V. Vail. 1974. *Lettuce Production in the United States.* Washington, D.C.: U.S. Dept. of Agriculture, Agricultural Handbook No. 221.

Winslow, Marj. 1976a. " 'Revolution' Likely in Lettuce Fields, " *The Packer,* April 10:19c. 1976b. "Revolution Hits California Fields: 'Green Army' Changes Techniques," *The Grower (Packer),* May 15:12b–13b.

Wolf, C. P. 1976. "Social Impact Assessment: The State of the Art Restated." *Sociological Practice, 1,* 1, Spring:56–70.

Zahara, M., S. S. Johnson, and R. E. Garrett. 1974. "Labor Requirements, Harvest Costs, and the Potential for Mechanical Harvest of Lettuce." *Journal of the American Society for Horticultural Science, 99,* 6, November:535–7.

Zahara, Mike, John H. MacGillivray, and Orval D. McCoy. 1960. *Labor Requirement of Lettuce Harvest in Imperial Valley.* Davis: University of California, Dept. of Vegetable Crops, Vegetable Crops Series 98.

Zahara, M., and O. D. McCoy. 1963. *Four Methods of Lettuce Harvest.* Davis: University of California, Dept. of Vegetable Crops, Vegetable Crops Series 130.

Index

adoption
 and diffusion, 96
 rate of, 108–10
agriculture
 and the capitalist mode of production, 6–7, 15
 as production system, 1–2
 and the state, 5–6
 See also sociology of agriculture
analytic foci, 32
Antle, Bud, 64, 77, 78–81, 83, 84, 88, 89, 102

bracero program, 25, 26, 37, 41, 91
braceros, 38, 41, 66
Burawoy, Michael, 3, 10, 19, 25, 135

California Tomato Growers Association, 44
capitalist form of production, 8
change
 incremental, 31, 35
 social, 27
 transformational, 31, 35–6
concentration, processes of, 38, 39, 46, 111–12
conflict, 9, 10, 18
control, 100–3
 and domination, 4, 9–11
crews, *see* harvesters

differentiation, 3, 15

family farm, 7
Finerman, Mel, 51–2, 80
firms, 74–81, 134
Fisher, Lloyd, 3, 24–6

growers, 15
 grower-shippers, 44, 49, 53, 74
 and organizations, 17–18
 organizations of lettuce, 81–5
 and patterns of production, 17

of tomatoes, 39–40
 social consequences of mechanical lettuce harvesting for, 111–12

harvesters
 ground pack, 58–61, 67–9, 115–16
 shredded lettuce, 63–5
 wrap pack, 61–3, 116
 see also labor force; lettuce, workers

industrial sociology, 2–3
 and labor process, 4

Johnson, Stanley S., 62, 71–3, 108–9, 112–13, 139, 141, 143

knowledge production, 6, 20–2, 28–30, 35

labor contractors, 58
labor force
 changes in composition of by mechanization, 115–17
 changes in post mechanization, 41
 changes in work organization of by mechanization, 118–21
 costs of, 29
 displacement of, by mechanization, 112–15, 139–43
 documented and undocumented, 11, 99–100, 115
 ethnicity of, 18
 externalized, 56, 57
 gender and, 18; greencard, 115
 internalized, 56
 numbers in, 51, 69–74, 108
 recruitment and organization of, 18
 reproduction of, 18
 semi-internalized, 58
 supply, 11, 37, 99, 100
 surplus, 56
 see also, harvesters; labor markets; lettuce, workers

157